A Hundred Years of the IAPR: A Celebratory Supplement to the *Archive for the Psychology of Religion*

Wilhelm Stählin, 1883-1975. Founding Editor of the Archive for the Psychology of Religion *and founder of the International Association for the Psychology of Religion*

A Hundred Years of the IAPR: A Celebratory Supplement to the *Archive for the Psychology of Religion*

Studies and Discussions of the History of the International Association for the Psychology of Religion

Edited by

Jacob A. Belzen

BRILL

LEIDEN | BOSTON

Library of Congress Cataloging-in-Publication Data

Names: Belzen, J. A. van (Jacob Adrianus), 1959- editor.
Title: A hundred years of the IAPR : a celebratory supplement to the Archive for the Psychology of Religion : studies and discussions of the history of the International Association for the Psychology of Religion / edited by Jacob A. Belzen.
Description: Leiden ; Boston : Brill, 2016. | Includes bibliographical references.
Identifiers: LCCN 2016021032 (print) | LCCN 2016021440 (ebook) | ISBN 9789004322004 (paperback : alk. paper) | ISBN 9789004322011 (E-book)
Subjects: LCSH: Psychology, Religious. | Internationale Gesellschaft f?ur Religionspsychologie--History. | Archiv f?ur Religionspsychologie (1962)
Classification: LCC BL53.A1 H86 2016 (print) | LCC BL53.A1 (ebook) | DDC 200.1/9--dc23
LC record available at https://lccn.loc.gov/2016021032

Typeface for the Latin, Greek, and Cyrillic scripts: “Brill”. See and download: brill.com/brill-typeface.

ISBN 978-90-04-32200-4 (paperback)
ISBN 978-90-04-32201-1 (e-book)

This book is printed on acid-free paper and produced in a sustainable manner.

Contents

Preface

In 2015, both the journal *Archive for the Psychology of Religion* and the International Association for the Psychology of Religion (IAPR), the bearer or owner of that journal, completed their first century. A centennial often is taken as the occasion for historical work on the scientific infrastructure concerned and for reflection on its cause or reason for existence. Also in the case of IAPR and *Archive*, an extensive study of their history has been taken as a point of departure for a discussion of fundamental issues in the psychology of religion more generally, asking questions like: What and how is this field doing? What is it about? Which factors play a role? Who are the practitioners? Whom does the (sub)discipline serve? What have been the place and value of the infrastructure now celebrating its anniversary? The report of the study has been publicly discussed at IAPR's biannual conference (Istanbul, Turkey, August 2015) and at some other occasions.

The present volume brings together a number of the contributions to these discussions, continues them and takes them further by making them more precise, adding new voices and responding to some criticism raised. Hopefully, these discussions will expand beyond this volume, which has been organized in close relationship to the *Archive for the Psychology of Religion* and follows its format. I gratefully acknowledge that the review of the contributions submitted for this volume has been arranged for by the present editorial team of that journal.

The metatheoretical discussions presented here belong to the segment of psychology usually called "history and foundations of psychology": they don't practice the psychology of religion themselves, but reflect on this (sub)discipline, and can only be conducted by such scholars equipped with embracing knowledge of the psychology of religion, its history, and its intellectual contexts. Each of the authors in this volume meets these requirements: trained in different academic disciplines, coming from a range of countries, and all well acquainted with IAPR's history or/and the history of psychology, religious studies, theology, or other fields neighboring to the psychology of religion, they present a variety of viewpoints and opinions in and on this subject.[1]

1 Unfortunately, for personal reasons, David M. Wulff (USA) had to withdraw from the project in its final stage. Wulff probably would have been in the best position to enter the discussions this volume presents, as he is widely read in European psychology of religion and for decades a key figure in US-psychology of religion.

The primary aim of such a reflective engaging in the history of an academic discipline like the psychology of religion is neither to produce a *communis opinion* nor to propose any definitive statements, but rather to bring different viewpoints to the fore and into discussion with one another, all the while proving that in academia being of different opinions does not preclude respect and collaboration (and sometimes even friendship). It is this spirit that hopefully will continue to characterize both IAPR and the *Archive for the Psychology of Religion*, now on their way into a second century!

Jacob A. Belzen
Amsterdam, December 21, 2015

Notes on Contributors

Lars Allolio-Näcke
PD Dr. phil. Dipl.-Psych, got his *venia legendi* for psychology of religion in January 2015. He is Director of the Center for "Anthropology of Religion(s)" at the Friedrich-Alexander-Universität Erlangen-Nürnberg, Germany. He is a member of the board of the Division "History" of the German Psychological Society.

Jacob A. Belzen
holds doctorates in social sciences, history, philosophy and sciences of religions (*Religionswissenschaften*). Since 1993, he is a full professor of psychology of religion at the University of Amsterdam. In the years 1992–2006, he served on IAPR's board, since 2001 as its President.

Jozef Corveleyn
was trained as a psychologist, a philosopher, and a psychoanalyst. After working for years as a clinician in a psychiatric hospital, he specialized in clinical psychology of religion, a subject he taught at the Departments for Psychology of both the Catholic University of Leuven (Belgium) and the (formerly Calvinistic) Free University Amsterdam. In the years 2006–2011, he served as President of IAPR.

Sarah Demmrich
studied psychology and theology at Martin Luther University Halle-Wittenberg and the psychology of religion at University of Vienna. She holds a PhD in Psychology (Martin Luther University Halle-Wittenberg) and works as an assistant professor for psychology with specialization in the psychology of religion at Süleyman Şah University, Istanbul, Turkey.

Nils G. Holm
studied theology, sciences of religion and psychology at Åbo Akademi University (Turku, Finland) and at Uppsala University (Sweden). As a professor of the sciences of religion (*Religionswissenschaften*) at Åbo Akademi University, he specialized in psychological approaches to the study of religions. A member of IAPR's board from 1984 to 2006, he served 1995–2001 as its President.

Erich Nestler

Dr. theol.habil., Dr. phil., MA/AGTS, Springfield, Dipl. Relpäd. (FH), retired in 2013 as faculty member (apl. Prof. for Practical Theology) at the department of Theology, University of Erlangen-Nuremberg and as religion teacher in the public school system. His doctoral dissertation was on Wilhelm Stählin, founder of both IAPR and ARP.

Troels Nørager

was trained in and graduated in systematic theology. Specializing in philosophy of religion, he is an associate professor at the Department of Culture and Society at Aarhus University (Denmark). He published extensively on the work of Villiam Grønbaek, IAPR's President between 1963 and 1969.

Herman Westerink

studied theology at Groningen University (The Netherlands), where he specialized in the domain of psychology and religion, an area for which he was appointed at Vienna University (Austria) between 2007 and 2013. He is a member of the Philosophy Department of the Radboud University (Nijmegen, Netherlands). In the years 2009–2013, he served as Secretary General-Treasure of IAPR.

Uwe Wolfradt

(PhD in Psychology, University of Osnabrück, PhD in Social Anthropology, University of Leipzig) is an associate professor for psychology at the Martin-Luther-University Halle-Wittenberg, Germany. He served as President of the Division "History" of the German Psychological Society.

Tania Zittoun

trained as a psychologist in Switzerland and the UK. She is a professor at the Institute of Psychology and Education at the University of Neuchâtel (Switzerland), specializing in cultural psychology.

CHAPTER 1

History for Theory: The International Association for the Psychology of Religion as an Empirical Basis for Reflection on the Discipline

Jacob A. Belzen

Summary

This chapter discusses whether, to which extent and in what way IAPR's history can serve as an empirical basis for reflection on some of the theoretic basic issues in the psychology of religion. Attention is given to some enduring problems facing the discipline and to some different types of psychology of religion. A new hypothesis is formulated about IAPR's founder suddenly leaving the field, followed by a brief introduction to the volume.

Introduction

We shall not cease from exploration
And the end of all our exploring
Will be to arrive where we started
And know the place for the first time.

T. S. ELIOT (1942), *Four quartets*, nr. 4, V

∵

An Easy Question for a not so Easy Beginning

If anyone asks how the psychology of religion is doing – what would be the correct answer be? Probably one would obtain very different answers, depending on whom, or in what kind of circles, the question is asked. Among psychologists, especially in Europe, there may be some amazement: They may never have heard about psychology of religion at all. Among historians of religion, someone may have heard about the older Freudian or Jungian approaches

 | DOI 10.1163/9789004322011_002

to the study of religion, or even about more recent ones like cognitive science of religion, but is that all there is to the field? And more important, how is that field doing? Among some observers, one certainly will hear critical things, e.g., from many theologians one will obtain the answer that psychology of religion was a movement at the beginning of the 20th century, long outdated by now; among other theologians, one will hear that psychology of religion doesn't exist, because it cannot exist: Religion being the result of divine activity, it is not accessible to an empirical science like psychology. And many more contradicting answers can be heard.

Obviously, the quality of the answer will depend on the quality of the reasoning underlying the answer, but for sure all kind of apriori's that hardly can be rationally accounted for will play a role, both in the answer and in its evaluation. Many of these apriori's may sound like axioms, they are based on other-than rational reasoning (e.g., sensitivities), but once given their deposition, reasoning founded on them may be quite rational. So, whom to listen to when asking how the psychology of religion is doing?

One question that needs to be clarified before any answer to that question is possible at all, is the question what the psychology of religion as such is. Yet, an answer to this question is almost as difficult to achieve as the answer to the previous question. For again, opinions and scholarly definitions may vary enormously and all kinds of factors play a role in the answering. As hardly needs to be pointed out here, opinions and definitions of both constitutive terms in the designation "psychology of religion" differ: What is religion to some, is no religion to others (Is Jihad religion? Is sacred sex a religious ritual? Was the Inquisition a religious institution? Practicing charity? Yoga?); there hardly is a term about whose definition exists as much controversy as "religion". When it comes to an understanding of "psychology", disagreement prevails equally: What is psychology to some, is no psychology to others. (Does Transpersonal Psychology belong to the science of psychology? Is psychoanalysis psychology?) And no less tricky is the little word "of" in the phrase "psychology of religion": What does that mean? Is psychology of religion a psychology that belongs to religion? Is it a psychology explicating what the human being is and how human beings function according to a given religion? Or does it explain how religious involvement functions, according to that religion? Or is the psychology of religion helping religion by means of psychology? So, e.g., providing knowledge to pastors and ecclesiastical functionaries about psychological functioning, enabling them to better or easier achieve whatever their goals may be? Or is psychology of religion those parts of psychology that deal with religion? If so, what would that mean, then? Is the construction of a scale to assess the importance of religious viewpoints in making everyday decisions an example of psychology of religion? Is a discussion of the possible role of religiosity in psychotherapy an example of psychology of religion? Is an investigation why certain religious denominations refuse psychological treatment to their members a study in the psychology of religion? Is writing on religious experiences an example of being involved in the psychology of religion?

Even without having said anything on the content level, our questioning has brought us an important insight: Asking for an answer as to how the psychology of religion is doing is likely to lead one into a jungle of opinions. As a composite phrase, "psychology of religion" is even far more pluriform than any of its constituent term in itself already is. Any definition given can be, and will have to be, questioned as to why this particular definition is given by this person at this time in this context. But to whom to grant the privilege of providing any definition of the psychology of religion at all?

To the last question there seem to be at least two classic and rather straightforward ways of answering. One is the systematic way: Ask an eminent psychologist of religion what psychology of religion is. For who would be in a better position to give the answer than an eminent psychologist of religion? It sounds logical, even simple, but it isn't: for how to know who is an eminent psychologist of religion? Very different views will exist as to whom to regard as such. But even if one would listen to one eminent psychologist of religion, spelling out her or his answer to the question, situating it in the necessary contexts, perhaps even comparing it to other answers, this "systematic" procedure would still only provide one answer. It would perhaps be a very sophisticated answer that this eminent psychologist of religion provides, but why listen to this psychologist of religion rather than to another, who puts forward a perhaps equally sophisticated but different answer? And there is no guarantee at all that any well-reasoned opinion, on any subject, will become prevalent. Take the preeminent thinker Kant (1724–1804): He provided a careful argumentation which led him to the conclusion that no scientific psychology is possible. Although acknowledging his importance and reading his works at nearly all universities, the Western world proceeded different than Kant wanted .... Concerning the psychology of religion Roscam Abbing (1914–1996), a professor from Groningen (The Netherlands), published some decades ago a very learned book, also dealing with its relationships to philosophy and theology (Roscam Abbing, 1981), but the book was so thick, that hardly anyone ever read it. Perhaps Roscam Abbing's treatise was superb, but what if the potential audience doesn't listen?

The other classic and seemingly straightforward way to an answer would be to ask all those who claim to be psychologists of religion what psychology of religion is and provide the greatest common divisor as a result. This "empirical" procedure has serious limitations too. For whom in fact to ask? Where to find all those that belong to the psychology of religion? Write to all associations for psychology? To all departments for psychology? To all departments and societies for religious studies? Or to all of these bodies, and perhaps to some more?[1] The procedure would probably provide a cacophony of opinions already hinted at, resulting in no simple and straightforward answer to the question what the psychology of religion is, let alone to how this enterprise is doing. For an enterprise it certainly is: Psychology of religion is not only an idea, it is not just what any definition says it is. Especially in the domain of psychology, that has so often claimed "behavior" to be its object of study, one should be aware that next to ideas and definitions, what has actually been done or presented as psychology of religion needs to be taken into consideration for an answer to that only seemingly simple question: How is the psychology of religion doing? We therefore need to know what psychologists of religion are or have been doing, what they achieved, where and how they practice, what do they have to offer, where do they receive their training, etc. And again we run into the same problem, for in order to try to find an answer, one needs already to have an answer, for without that answer one wouldn't even know where to look for an answer.

A clear case of circular reasoning, so it seems! And indeed it is, but this does not necessary indicate logical flaw. We are dealing here with a case of the so-called hermeneutical circle, as discussed by philosophers like Gadamer: When searching for insight, one seems to go through circles, one has a notion (a *Vorverständnis*) of what one is searching for, one enters an inquiry, will be sometimes be confirmed, but also contradicted, perhaps corrected, hopefully eventually be guided towards a better insight (*Horizontverschmelzung*). As such, the search for an answer never really stops, as any new constellation, e.g., new information becoming accessible, may require a new assessment, a new making up one's mind, resulting perhaps in modification. No direct line, but a meandering one is what the search for insight is like – to what extent ever ideologies, bad journalism, and shouting commercials may prefer one-liners.

Where Do We Find the Psychology of Religion?

All of this reasoning should help to make us cautious: Easy answers are to be suspected! But again, where to obtain any answer at all? Where to find the

1 One probably wouldn't turn to departments for English language and literature, or would one? Not doing so, would make one miss important work like Mel D. Faber's, however (see, e.g., his 2002, 2004, 2010).

practitioners of the psychology of religion? Where to turn to if we want to see what psychologists of religion have been doing? Perhaps – really perhaps!, the adequacy of this potential option will need to be discussed – an organization specific for the psychology of religion would be a good beginning? Given that there seems to be no canon in the psychology of religion, no common opinion, no accreditation of any kind specific to the psychology of religion, such an organization could indeed be a starting point. Which one to choose then? The largest organization for, or by the name, "psychology of religion", is probably Division 36 of the very influential American Psychological Association (APA). But, as important as the APA is in the world of international psychology, this organization covers not much more than the USA, and the division by the name for psychology of religion only originated in 1976 (although a forerunner was founded in 1948[2]). By 1976 psychology of religion existed for quite a time already, however, if we take publications by that title as an indication of the existence of a scientific discipline by that name.[3] Even stronger: Many of those that are remembered as founding fathers of present day psychology (like Fechner, Wundt, James, Freud, Hall, Janet, and many others) also contributed to the psychology of religion literature. So, whatever its features or qualities, the field being far older than 1976 or even 1948, we better choose another organization – if we want to stay with an organization – than APA's Div. 36.

2 To be more precise (which is not easy, as one finds different years mentioned in the literature): More or less in 1948 the American Catholic Psychological Association was founded, a kind of a satellite organization to the APA. Its name changed in 1970 to Psychologists Interested in Religious Issues (PIRI), in 1976 it became an official division of the APA (number 36) (Kugelmann, 2011, pp. 274–289; Malony, 2015, p. 45–46; Reuder, 1999). In 1993 the name was changed to Psychology of Religion, in 2012 the division became The Society for the Psychology of Religion and Spirituality. Since 2009, this society publishes the journal *Psychology of Religion and Spirituality*; APA since 2014 also publishes a journal *Spirituality in Clinical Practice*.

3 Note that a publication by the name "x" does not necessary indicate, not even in hindsight, that a discipline "x" exists. In 1997, a monography with "Paranormologie" in the title was published (Resch, 1997). Does it mean that "paranormology" as a science exist? In 1899, the very first monography with the title *Psychology of Religion* was published (Starbuck, 1899), but the phrase "psychology of religion" seems to have used the first time by the professor of dogmatics and moral theology Henrik Reuterdahl (1837) and according to the well-informed Vorbrodt (1926, p. 91), it was G. Stanley Hall who first lectured on "psychology of religion" in 1881. And on the other hand: Does the absence of the phrase "psychology of religion" indicate that a work does not belong to the psychology of religion? What about the *Attempt at a theory about religious insanity* by the German psychiatrist Ideler? His lengthy book was published in two volumes, the titles to be translated as *The Features of Religious Insanity* (Ideler, 1848) and *The Development of Religious Insanity* (Ideler, 1850). A much later, internationally acknowledged highlight in the literature such as Vergote's *Guilt and Desire* (1978/1988) does not go by the title "psychology of religion" either.

There certainly have been other, even older organizations, but they need not all be mentioned here. Let us, for once, go short: There is an organization in the psychology of religion that exists (or seems to exist – don't expect things to become simple!) since 1914.[4] There is no other organization for the psychology of religion that is older than this one, at present called "International Association for the Psychology of Religion" (IAPR). There is also no other organization that would be or has been more international than IAPR. In some ways, therefore, this association could opt as a fair candidate for an exploration of what the psychology of religion is and has been doing. The history of this organization could well provide an insight into what kind of discussions have been going on in the psychology of religion, what kinds of subjects have been dealt with, what kind of problems needed to be surmounted, etc. A focus on this organization could turn the *mer-à-boire* hinted at above into a manageable project: Instead of endlessly deliberating whom or what to discuss or not, the subjects to be treated would be limited, in principle, to what happened in the context of this organization. And as not all too much is known about the past of this organization, its completing a first century of existence in 2015 seems to legitimize a study of its history: Who belonged to this organization at all? What did it ever achieve? Why did it perish or at least seem to perish repeatedly? How did it, or its members, define the psychology of religion? Even if an immense labor, answers to such questions might be achievable within a certain limit of time.

An undertaking as this has clear limits too, however. Even before beginning: What guarantee do we have that we have chosen the best object for research? Did all, or at least most, of the most important (or best known?) psychologists of religion ever belong to this association? In what way is it representative of "the" psychology of religion? Do not the discontinuities in its existence disqualify the organization as an object for more theoretically oriented reflections as to how the psychology of religion is doing and what kind of enterprise it is? (Or are perhaps such discontinuities indications of discontinuities in the field

4 The organization was established in 1914 to support the new research outlet *Archiv für Religionspsychologie* (*Archive for the Psychology of Religion*), which was meant by its founding editor Wilhelm Stählin to replace the older *Zeitschrift für Religionspsychologie* (*Journal for Psychology of Religion*), which was published between 1907 and 1913, and which was at least partly inspired by the *American Journal for Religious Psychology and Education*, founded by G. S. Hall and published between 1904 and 1915. In many respects, mainly due to World War I, 1914 was also the end of both the organization and the *Archiv für Religionspsychologie*. In 1928–1929 the organization was revived, only to perish again in the 1930s. A kind of formal reconstitution took place in 1960, a reorganization in 2001 saved it from another extinction (Belzen, 2015).

as such? Without engaging in actual empirical historical research we will have no answer to such questions.) And the great risk is that focusing on the history of this particular organization closes the eyes to what has been going on outside the organization, which may both quantitatively and qualitatively have been and perhaps still be much more important that what happened and happens within the organization.

Scholarship's Essential Virtue: Modesty

Taking all advantages and disadvantages into consideration, being limited in many ways (like access to a number of sources in Europe, but hardly outside of the core of this continent), the study *Religionspsychologie. Eine historische Analyse im Lichte der Internationalen Gesellschaft* (*Psychology of Religion. A Historical Analysis in the Light of Its International Association*; Belzen, 2015) has tried to counter the risks hinted at: it provides an analysis of what has happened within the IAPR, all the while comparing with and providing information about the (international) context. In this way, the study constitutes in no way a history of "the" psychology of religion, but it does provide an element of such a history, on which other researchers can build or which they can amend, criticize, extend, employ, or whatever may serve their purposes.

The aim of the study has been to deal with some fundamental questions about the psychology of religion: what kind of an enterprise is it, what did it achieve, what can one realistically expect from it, what kinds of problems are encountered, how is that field doing, and so on. The empirical object that it provides some detailed information about is the International Association for the Psychology of Religion and its medium the *Archiv für Religionspsychologie* (*Archive for the Psychology of Religion*). Within the variety of views in and on the psychology of religion, IAPR's *Sitz im Leben* is limited – but so would be any other object of historical inquiry as an empirical basis for reflections on the psychology of religion.

Both author and reader of the research report that large parts of the study *Religionspsychologie* in fact are, should also be aware of the limitations of the researcher. Someone who has been actively involved himself in an association like IAPR for over thirty years may not be the best candidate to do a history of that organization. Or perhaps such a person is indeed the best candidate? Without in-depth knowledge of the field of psychology of religion (but what is that?) just any member of the organization may not qualify for research on history. One certainly will need to bring specific knowledge and most of all expertise in historical scholarship, also in its empirical branch, to come up with results that were not yet known or with opinions that have not already been voiced over and over. And the same could be said about factors like nationality, mother tongue, affiliation, and some more: Being born and in the main trained in the Netherland and functioning from that country may be an advantage when turning to a history that played essentially in German speaking European countries. It could equip one with a fresh look, asking questions that other foreigners would also pose, it could make one alert to issues or sentiments a native researcher would be blind to or be embarrassed about. It *could* be that way, but it could also be the other way round: Perhaps being a foreigner prevents understanding some developments, because of lack of background knowledge? What has been the case in the study *Religionspsychologie*, and what the quality of the research reported and of the reflections offered is, will have to be judged upon by others, a beginning with which is made in the present volume.

As attractive or well-argued the idea of such a piece of research may be, its systematic implementation is always accompanied by inherent disadvantages, both for the author and for the reader. The amount of work that needs to be invested in the case of such a piece of research is immense: As IAPR does not have an archive of its own, one tediously needs to set out on a journey to possible sources of information, which in the case of such an international organization may be scattered all over Europe and beyond. And there never is the guarantee that there would not be a very rich, even important source of information somewhere that would throw a very different light on all kinds of development that one needs to deal with. Also, proceeding in a strict way, limiting oneself to the route outlined in an introductory chapter of the research report, may well mean that one needs to deal with all kinds of literature, events and persons one does not like oneself. And on the other hand it may imply that all kinds of literature, events and persons one holds in high esteem, cannot be dealt with. And one also needs to be aware, apriori, of the risks of being misunderstood, despite having laid out carefully how modest one's intentions, how small of the research and how limited the possibilities have been. To a large extent, this is always the case when publishing the results of any systematic piece of research: one runs the risk of readers asking precisely for such information as one has carefully argued for *not* to provide. There will always be readers asking why one did not discuss this or that author, why one did not give more attention to this or that they think is important, why one did not deal with their heroes or – unpardonable sin! – talk more about themselves ...[5] The

5 When I published a study of the psychology of religion in the Netherlands (Belzen, 2007), I took the only special aspect of the situation in the Netherlands as a guideline. Leaving to

only way to safeguard oneself from these of criticisms is probably to never publish.

Some Problems Facing the Psychology of Religion

As indicated, the aim of the study *Religionspsychologie* was to reflect on the psychology of religion. As it is impossible to summarize the study here (for a very brief overview, see the next chapter of the present volume), just mentioning of some issues dealt with should suffice. Taking a look at the (history of the) psychology of religion, some problems the discipline struggles with readily present themselves. Let us only briefly consider just three of them: instrumentalization, overestimation, and inflation (see also Belzen, 2016).

1. An important key to almost any oeuvre on religion, is the personal religious stand of the author: the position taken (sometimes even without being aware of having taken such a stand) is highly influential throughout his or her entire writings. Although most authors present their work as "objective", formulating as distanced as possible, it should not really come as a surprise that the form of religion they practice themselves or that they consider to be the best, makes its presence felt in the conclusions of their analysis. In other words, what is offered as an objective, neutral, "scientific" psychological analysis of religion is actually influenced in some prejudicial way by the author's private views. While countless examples could be given, we will confine ourselves to but a few obvious ones from different periods of time. At the dawn of the 20th century, Jean Du Buy concluded, on the basis of the "stages" he distinguished in the phylogenetic and ontogenetic development of mankind, the following hierarchical order among the world's religions: Islam, Confucianism, Christianity, Buddhism, and Vedic (Indian) philosophy. Within Christianity his ranking was: Calvinism, Methodism, Baptism, and Unitarianism – all of which, we should note, perfectly correlated with the religious ideas of G. Stanley Hall (1846–1924), the supervisor of DuBuy's doctoral dissertation. Over fifty years

others to assess whatever the value of Dutch contributions to the psychology of religion may have been, I choose to analyze the somewhat remarkable institutionalization of the discipline in this small country: In 2000, there were 11 professorships, of different kinds, plus a good number of other academic positions assigned to the psychology of religion, a seemingly privileged situation as existed in no other country. But even kind reviewers complained that I did not talk enough about William James (who never had anything to do with Dutch institutionalization of the psychology of religion, though) or that I did not discuss Jan van Baal (1909–1992), a very interesting professor in cultural anthropology, who never published under the title psychology of religion, never saw himself as a psychologist of religion, and by no one ever was regarded as a psychologist of religion (Nauta, 2011; Vergeer, 2008).

later, Gordon Allport (1897–1967) had been puzzled by the high correlation between religiosity and prejudice as found in many empirical studies; he restored his peace of mind by introducing the distinction between intrinsic and extrinsic religiosity: Extrinsic religiosity would correlate high with vices like prejudice, intrinsic wouldn't (Allport & Ross, 1967); when C. Daniel Batson (*1943) some decades later expanded this typology by empirically assessing a third type ("quest-religiosity"), this type proved to be a fair rendering of his own religiosity (Batson & Ventis, 1982). According to the contemporary psychologist Bering (*1975), a confessing atheist, psychology explains why religious belief is wrong (Bering, 2010). Yet according to his antipode, the evangelical Christian Justin Barrett (*1971), psychology shows that being religious is the default setting of the human being, while result of our divine creation (Barrett, 2011). One could hardly have two more opposed conclusions!

To go short: All kinds of religious stands have been formulated employing scientific psychological theory and/or research. Although almost anyone at present will admit that no science can ever prove or disprove any religious claim (as science and religion are about different ontological domains), the private stand of psychologists of religion has been shaping their work heavily, also in the work of those sincerely striving for religious neutrality. Even in the work of present day theorists explicitly striving for neutrality, like Antoine Vergote (1921–2013) or David Wulff (*1940), their private religious preferences are noticeable. In general, one can say that psychology largely has been "instrumentalized": It is used to argue in favor of the religious stand of this or that particular author.

2. Whether as such strongly or mildly religiously inspired, ever since the rise of modern psychology, people have put forward great expectations towards it. As regards religion, the "turn to the subject", the recognition of human factors being at work, had its forerunners in such important thinkers as Descartes, Kant, and Schleiermacher. Historians of philosophy usually see the onset of Modernity with René Descartes (1596–1650). The emphasis on epistemology within contemporary philosophy finds its origin in his thought, which had the effect of putting the experiencing subject at the heart of philosophical considerations. By the 18th century numerous factors combined to consider thinking of the world without God or divine efficacy a viable option. With Kant (1724-1804), the so-called anti-metaphysical twist implemented itself: Subject and object were definitely separated from each other and objective knowledge could only be called into question, which greatly weakened the normative character of Christian dogma. A new way of looking at religion came up: Instead of being an obligation towards God, it became a human need, instead of a revelation it became a human phenomenon. Many later commentators

have seen here a turning point: Theology changed from being knowledge of God towards religious anthropology and history of religions.

At the same time, it should be noted that such acknowledgement of human factors in religion was by no means anti-religious. None of the three just mentioned thinkers was anti-religious, on the contrary: Friedrich Schleiermacher (1768–1834), for example, defended religion to be a natural characteristic of the human being. He did not see religion as a subordinate place in the mind or the will, but secured it an "independent province in the mind". Religion should be understood "neither as thinking nor as acting, but as contemplation and feeling." Religion would have to do with susceptibility, with "sense and taste for the infinite" (Schleiermacher, 1799/1821). Schleiermacher connected human self-consciousness and religion intimately: Human beings, aware of their finitude, feeling depending on and integrated into a larger whole, would as such be religious.

Throughout the 20th century, during which psychology increasingly began to become itself a distinct academic discipline, expectations towards psychology grew still further: the discipline would not only investigate psychic functioning, but also contribute to enhancing health, enable better human relationships, help to achieve peace among the nations, and what have you. (The APA, the world's largest organization for psychology, explicitly states that it aims to advance psychology in order to benefit society and to improve people's lives.)

Granted, at the beginning of the 1900s in religiously conservative, especially Roman Catholic, circles, there was still outright fear of psychology. (Religious leaders foresaw that psychology would lead to apostasy and secularization.) But in liberal, especially Protestant, circles, psychology was embraced as the remedy to the problems the Christian Church was confronted with: Psychology would teach clergy to take the human situation into account, framing the message of the Gospel in a form comprehensible to citizens of a Western, modernizing society. Bloodless dogmatic theology should be psychologized (as church historian Scheel summarized 1908 the claims of many in the well-known German *Journal for Theology and Church*); the "misery of our scholarly supported faith teaching" would be rejuvenated by psychoanalysis (as Swiss pastor Pfister – after whom the American Psychiatric Association named one of its awards – stated in 1905); disciplines like history and philosophy would remain respectable, but only psychology would really enable religion to unfold its beneficial potential for present day human beings (as psychiatrist Bresler, founder of the first German *Journal for the Psychology of Religion*, formulated in 1907). One of the expectations of those interested in a psychological treatise on religion was that finally psychology would be able to explain religion as such: History as an academic discipline would only describe what had been the case, but psychology would explain *why* something had been the case! "No end to psychology", "to psychology the place of honor", and more titles like these headed theological publications in Germany in the 1920s and 1930s (Belzen, 1996).

Numerous psychologists of religion have tried to account for the existence of religion and its course in human history, whether they were presumably neutral, positive, or critical about religion themselves, as was the case with founding fathers like Wundt, Runze, and Freud respectively. Wilhelm Wundt (1932–1920) famously developed two different types of psychology, one modelled after the natural sciences, striving by experimental research on selected individuals to detect laws of psychological functioning, and one modelled after the humanities, striving to understand psychologically cultural phenomena irreducible to anyone's individual functioning. To the latter category belonged phenomena like ethics, customs, human society as such, and also religion. The human psyche's part in the development of religion as a non-individual cultural phenomenon, at work in the different historical types of religion, would be the function of phantasy, according to Wundt (1905). The philosopher and historian of religion Georg Runze (1852–1938), teaching at the Berlin theological faculty and principle editor of the first German *Journal for the Psychology of Religion,* viewed religion as the outgrowth of the human will to live, "the astonished admiration that we live, that the world exists, that being is", as he, romantically, formulated (Runze, 1894, p. 1). Skeptical about religion himself but never reducing it to any single psychological function, Sigmund Freud (1856–1939) penned several quite critical accounts about it, also in the forerunner of the *Archive for the Psychology of Religion,* detecting in religion psychological mechanisms like longing for protection by, but also fear of, a powerful father, and others, at work (Freud, 1907, 1913/1964, 1927/1961).

Throughout the entire history of the psychology of religion this tendency to explain religion by reference to its psychological roots has remained visible. Although many present day psychologists of religion, more or less modest, restrict themselves to commenting only on that (oftentimes very limited) aspect of religion or religiosity they happened to have been doing research on, some of the most eloquent representatives of evolutionary psychology, neuropsychology and especially "cognitive scientists of religion" (the latter group usually being theologians or religious scholars acquainted with these types of psychology) pretend again – or still! – to be able to explain religion *tout court,* whether neutrally, affirmatively or critically, from human psychological functions.

3. There is yet a third problem for the psychology of religion – but in fact for the psychology of any subject – which looks like just the reverse of the overestimation of psychology or of the exaggerated expectations of what this discipline can achieve. Bluntly stated: the apparent lack of progress in psychology. Obviously, this is not something psychologists like to hear about. The spread of psychological parlance throughout Western society and the ever continuing growth in number of psychologists, of publications, of research projects, and of grants available are usually presented as indications of the progress being achieved. But when Philipp Zimbardo (*1933) – thanks to his presence in the public media, probably the best known US-psychologist – answered the question "Does psychology make a significant difference in our lives?" a few years ago with an enthusiastic "yes!", he could refer only to psychological knowledge developed before the Second World War (Zimbardo, 2004). Despite much pep talk about psychology as presented in the various kinds of advertising of the American Psychological Association, theoretically oriented psychologists voice skepticism with regard to the question of progress.

Some time ago, celebrating the first centennial of psychology, *A Century of Psychology As a Science* was published. It took as its beginnings the installation of Wilhelm Wundt's room for experimental research at Leipzig University (which to some seems more like a political statement than a fair historical account). In this volume important and well-known psychologists reflected on their branch of science. It did not lead to much enthusiasm, however. The following quotation by Henry Gleitman (*1925), author of one of most used textbooks in psychology, is fairly representative:

> I do not know whether we have progressed much beyond [Wundt]. Our techniques are more sophisticated, and there are many more of us, so we can inundate each other in a mass of facts. But much of what we now do and think was already implicit in Wundt, and in other nineteenth century figures. We could do worse than to go back for an occasional glance at our intellectual origins … (Gleitman, 1985, p. 434)

Since then, psychologists taking a step back from concrete research projects and publishing, in order to assess the field as a whole, often have lamented the course of present day psychology: impressive quantitative growth, but hardly any theoretical progress. (Compare a title like *Methodological Thinking in Psychology: 60 Years Gone Astray?*, Toomela & Valsiner, 2010).

To be sure, different kinds of progress need to be distinguished: That at the moment more types of psychology than just psychoanalysis, clinical, and social psychology – approaches that have dominated the psychology of religion during most of the 20th century – are being employed in research on religion, may and should count as a kind of progress. Also, in present day psychology of religion a larger variety of religions, or more concretely, of religious forms of life are being explored than during most of the 20th century, which may and should certainly count as a kind of progress too: Whereas most older psychology of religion was about North-American Christianity, nowadays also other types of Christianity (e.g. Orthodox, or Asian American), specific populations (like prisoners, gays and lesbians, health care workers), and other religions (like Islamic, Buddhist, or Hindu traditions) come into focus. Finally, the turning away from predominantly working with college students to involving other types of subjects (like children, senior citizens, or Inuit) involved in real-life situations helps to validate psychological instruments (like theories and techniques for research or therapy) in additional contexts (Pargament, 2013). When performed in the field of religion, this clearly contributes to progress within the psychology of religion too. Yet, all of this is more an expansion of psychology (of religion) than development of new or better psychology.

Obviously, if such lament over the lack of theoretical progress in psychology in general is correct, this has consequences for the psychology of religion too. For psychology of religion relies on psychology in general: Psychology of religion is practiced by means of the same theoretical and empirical instruments as developed in psychology at large. The rise and development of a new approach in the psychology of religion is always dependent on a new type of psychology being developed and subsequently being applied in research and reflection on religion. How could it be different? Tautologically as it sounds, psychology of religion is psychology, psychology of religion depends on psychology. (And, to be honest, and therefore modest, it is not the other way round: Application in the field of religion has, much to the chagrin of some psychologists of religion, never been a condition for any type of psychology to arise and flourish.) Therefore, there is a problem here: If psychology as such does, despite growth, not progress theoretically, how could psychology of religion do so?

But, perhaps, the question as to progress in the psychology can be discussed from still another angle? Does not the plurality found in the field prompt a different approach to the question we set out with?

Different Types of Psychology of Religion

The varieties of understandings of what psychology and of what religion is or should be and of what the relationship between them is or can be is well reflected in the piece of history that presents itself in the past of the International Association for the Psychology of Religion. Acknowledging such pluriformity does not exclude taking a stand or preferring some kind of work over another nor does it imply any cowardly fear of choosing. It does preclude the possibility, however, of claiming that there would be only a single type of psychology of religion, it even excludes the possibility of talking about "the" psychology of religion. There are many psychologies of religion, and from a meta-perspective, one could even distinguish diverse types of psychology of religion. Which one is preferred by authors x or y will depend on all kinds of determinants like the training they have received, their religious apriori's, their institutional basis, the audiences they address and some more. With regard to our initial question, it leads to the somewhat puzzling finding that what seems to be progress according to one possible position within the discussion, may precisely indicate a lack of progress according to another position.

In an effort to grant the right of existence to the variety among the psychologies of religions, one could distinguish a threefold program:

1. The inclusion of religion, in what sense ever understood, in psychological reasoning and acting. Although this program is comprehensive – one could think of many types of research and application of psychological expertise – it could be called a "weak program", as the emphasis is not with the analysis of phenomena, events and situations called religious, but rather with either Theoretical Psychology (e.g., focusing on the relationship between psychology and religion – an important issue that as such does not seem to belong to the core of the psychology of religion), or the development or application of some psychological theory or technique (e.g., in the case of bringing religious variables or populations into the scope of a piece of empirical psychological research). In the latter case, the focus is on the development of psychological instruments (concepts or techniques) that might, but need not be, applied to religion. Paradoxically, and pointedly, expressed: This would be a type of psychology of religion that is not primarily concerned with religion, but with psychology. Research on religion functions here as a possible *application and illustration* of a particular psychological theory or technique.

2. The second program in the psychology of religion, however, has its focus with the *exploration* of religious phenomena, events and situations. This "strong program" can be seen as including all those efforts to explore, and possibly explain, empirical constellations considered religious in the light of a certain psychology. The biggest difference – even if it sometimes is more an accent than a principal difference – with the previous program is that the starting point is with religion (in what way ever understood), not with a psychological approach or method. By consequence, in such a piece of research even diverse

psychological theories or techniques may be employed, or psychological viewpoints may be combined with ones drawing on other scientific approaches (like anthropology, history or sociology). In such works one often encounters an interplay of extensive empirical description and multiple theory.

3. As a third program one could then consider all such efforts to determine or even explain religion, *tout court*, including its origin, development and reason of existence, by means of any psychology. This program is the oldest one in the psychology of religion and also the most theoretical one. It has had many precursors that from a contemporary perspective belong to the history of the philosophy of religion, from the efforts to explain religion as the result of fear of death in antiquity to the notion of religion as a socially produced illusion by Karl Marx (1818–1883). Ever since its introduction into thinking about religion, this program has attracted considerable attention, especially in its psychoanalytic variant, not only by scholars of all kinds, but up until today also by the general public (see bestselling books like Dawkins [2006], Dennett [2006], or Hitchens [2007], who often employ some type of popularizing or sometimes even vulgarizing psychology). The goal here is to arrive at an *explanation* why religion exists at all, which is clearly beyond psychology's sole competence, however, turning this program into an "all-too-strong" one.

Obviously, what counts as an advantage in one program, or to one observer, may resemble a disadvantage in another program or to another observer. Research as figuring in the weak program, striving to remain close to mainstream psychology and to get its results published in such journals, may be best recognizable as present day psychology and may facilitate the return of religion into the scope of the discipline of psychology at large. But it often has not too much to say about the religious phenomenon that functions as an illustration to the psychological theory or technique employed, and for that reason is often a disappointment to people interested in what psychology might have to say about religion (Nørager, 1996). This type of psychology of religion is therefore most attractive to and usually practiced by psychologists only, and the recent growth of the psychology of religion is probably owed to this program. Psychological reasoning as found with the third program is most attractive to people with strong theoretical interests, but it easily runs the risk of becoming a kind of vulgarized psychology, especially when "too much is explained by too little", sometimes even leading again to a type of ontological reductionism, when all of religion is derived from psychological mechanisms only. This type of psychology of religion is often enough no longer recognizable to research psychologists, as hardly any empirical investigation is reported here and the discussion is highly conceptual and goes into the direction of general theoretical debates about the relationship between psychology and religion in general. (In the main, such discussions are not found among psychologists, but among theologians and academics at institutes for religious studies [Jonte-Pace & Parsons, 2001], more often than not only engaging psychoanalysis, yet sometimes leading to excellent publications in their own right, see, e.g., Dixon, 1999; Parsons, 1999, 2013; Westerink, 2012.) The second program is one to which both experts of religion (like historians of religion, or comparative religionists, but also empirically oriented Christian theologians) and researchers drawing on a variety of approaches contribute. Not new psychology, but new psychological insight into something religious is what counts here, but it may, according to representatives of the first program, result in eclecticism and lack of scientific rigor, and it runs the risk, according to representatives of the third program, of presenting *Bilderbuchphänomenologie* (an academic swear word, which means something like: a book full of nice pictures, but failing to offer coherent analysis or overarching theory). Yet, the second program is radically empirical in its own way, for instead of molding an empirical phenomenon into the categories of some existing psychology (like often happening in the first program), it will concentrate on that empirical phenomenon and look whether existing psychologies have something to offer to its exploration (and perhaps explanation) at all. If need be, representatives of the second program will even prefer to device new ways of conducting empirical research rather than "subjecting" (mind the word!) religious people to standardized techniques as already developed in many other branches of psychology.

A More Excellent Way Than Psychology of Religion?

Having gone through part of the history of the field, leaves one also with some paradoxical findings, that prompt some other than theoretical reflections. In a volume on theoretical aspects of the psychology of religion coming to the fore through a study of IAPR's history, it may be appropriate to articulate one such finding about the very founder of both IAPR and the *Archive for the Psychology of Religion*.

As a young pastor, Wilhelm Stählin (1886–1975) was primarily interested in, as he called it, "the human being's reality and his [sic] world" (Stählin, 1968, p. 59), not so much in subjects like systematic theology or church history. An older colleague drew his attention to psychology, a subject that was fairly new in those days, and for which hardly any independent training existed. (In Germany, most early psychologists had a formal appointment as philosopher or psychiatrist.) Stählin grew so interested that he went back to the university for a second training: in "experimental psychology" (as it was understood in those days, which is quite different from its present understanding) and he finally become a doctor, not of theology, but of philosophy, qualifying himself with an empirically founded thesis as an experimental psychologist in the tradition of the famous Würzburg School in psychology. Very quickly he developed into one the most eloquent and best-known psychologists of religion in Germany (and probably in all of Europe), advocating an empirical approach and founding infrastructure for the discipline. He established contacts, both privately and on behalf of his *Archive*, with many leading psychologists of the day – only to leave the field suddenly in about 1916.

What had happened? Although there is not yet a definitive answer to this question – for which an in-depth study of his biography would be required – the following hypothesis could be given of what perhaps is a pervasive pattern in the psychology of religion. (A future researcher may want to assess whether such a pattern really can be distinguished.)

Being drawn to psychology because of his interest in "the human being's reality", Stählin studied the experimental psychology of his day. He learnt to be critical about other, non-experimental types of psychology. But then he ran into the publications of Max Scheler (1874–1928). Scheler inaugurated "philosophical anthropology", a new field in philosophy, into which he wanted to integrate results from empirical disciplines like sociology and psychology as indispensable for real insight into the human condition. He even tried to develop a phenomenological psychology. As is well known, phenomenological psychology is striving precisely for what was Stählin's interest: exploration of the "the human being's reality and his [sic] world" – to a much greater extent than experimental psychology can ever do. (To the essence of experimental approach it belongs to isolate some aspects of the object of study and to investigate it outside of its "world": in the standardized setting of a laboratory, where variables and conditions of the phenomenon may be manipulated. In contrast to an experience-near "phenomenological" approach, such analyzing, "dissecting" experimental approach is usually regarded as experience distant.)

Stählin must have been struck with phenomenology, as practiced by Scheler (1912, 1913–16/1921)[6]. He realized that he might have studied the wrong approach within psychology. Or even more seriously, that all of psychology, always essentially limited to only partial insight in any phenomenon, may not be the best way to get in touch with "the human being's reality and his [sic] world". What we do know, is that Stählin left psychology in its experimental version, that he developed an outright preference for phenomenological approaches, but that

6 Note: This was *before* Scheler started his famous criticism of the psychology of religion of his time.

he never got himself involved with empirical phenomenological psychology or with any phenomenological research in general. Rather, with his initial background as a pastor, he developed an interest of getting practically involved with religious reality, serving as a clergyman, as a leader of the *Wandervögel* (a youth movement searching for new ways of education), giving fair attention to the corporeal dimension of human life (so, integrating a good deal of sports, which counted as modern in those days), and striving for a renaissance of holistic spirituality.

What is important to note, however, is that the case of Stählin can be somewhat generalized. All through the history of the psychology of religion, we have had some of the most important representatives of the field commenting on its limited access to the religious life of human subjects and on the limits of what it can account for. Gordon Allport, who was so important in reviving the psychology of religion after World War II, concluded by the end of his career: "If we ask what psychology has contributed to our understanding of the religious nature of man, the answer is 'Less then we might wish'" (Allport, 1955, p. 93). Many promising scholars in the psychology of religion left the field at some point in their life. Like Stählin, they have chosen other life paths that allowed for far closer intimacy to the "the human being's reality and his [sic] world" than the necessarily limited approach of any science. While examples abound, it should suffice to mention two figures representing some totally different approaches within recent psychology of religion. After having developed into probably the most important European psychologist of religion after WW II (Vergote, 1978/1988, 1983/1996), Antoine Vergote, since his retirement, has contributed to his discipline only on explicit invitation. He has chosen instead to turn his attention to subjects that have been higher on his private agenda and which are of a philosophical and theological nature (like Vergote, 1998, 1999, 2007). Ralph Hood (*1942) certainly belongs to the internationally best-known US-psychologists of religion, having gained himself an impressive reputation for empirical work in the positivistic-empirical tradition, especially on mysticism (Hood, 2001). Gradually, however, he turned to empirical work of a much more descriptive, folkloristic type, allowing him to get much more directly in touch with human religious life (Hood & Williamson, 2008; Poloma & Hood, 2008).

The Present Volume

IAPR and the *Archiv für Religionspsychologie* completing their first century in 2015, and both being more alive and in better shape than perhaps ever before, the present supplement to the *Archive for the Psychology of Religion* deals with some aspects of their history.

Concurring with the introduction, the volume offers a broad perspective of possible approaches to working on the history of the field. Like "the" psychology of religion does not exist, "the" (published) history of that field does not exist either. What does exist, is a multiplicity of perspectives and of happenings and constellations probably of interest to anyone wanting to know more about the enterprise called "psychology of religion". As the reader will see, some of the authors of the chapters following the introduction take the publication of *Religionspsychologie* as their point of departure, offering comments, criticism, suggestions for additional research, and so on. They come from a variety of backgrounds, a variety as typically found in the psychology of religion, and certainly in IAPR, both in its history and its present: There are articles by psychologists, theologians, and religious scholars. There are articles by systematic theologians (such as Nørager and Westerink), some of which turned into empirical researchers themselves (like Nestler); there are articles by historians of psychology (like Wolfradt); there are articles by psychologists who function at departments for psychology (like Demmrich), but also by such psychologists who made a career in the context of theology or of religious studies (like Allolio-Näcke). There are articles by insiders (past presidents Corveleyn, Holm) and by outsiders (Zittoun) to the International Association for the Psychology of Religion. In the last article, there is a response to the remarks made about *Religionspsychologie* (Belzen). And note: Many of the authors mentioned only once could figure in several of the categories just distinguished.

It is quite a variety that is offered here, and still only a fraction of what would be necessary for an embracing history of "the" psychology of religion that might serve as an empirical basis for theoretical reflection on this academic enterprise. At least, some valuable elements for such an undertaking have been brought together here as a worthy entry into IAPR's second century.

References

Allport, G.W. (1955). *Becoming: Basic considerations for a psychology of personality*. New Haven, CT: Yale University Press.

Allport, G.W., & Ross, J.M. (1967). Personal religious orientation and prejudice. *Journal of Personality and Social Psychology, 5*, 432–443.

Barrett, J.L. (2011). *Cognitive science, religion and theology: From human minds to divine minds*. West Conshohocken, PA (USA): Templeton Press.

Batson, C.D., & Ventis, W.L. (1982). *The religious experience: A social-psychological perspective*. New York: Oxford University Press.

Belzen, J. A. (1996). Die blühende deutsche Religionspsychologie der Zeit vor dem Zweiten Weltkrieg und eine niederländische Quelle zur Geschichte der deutschen Psychologie. In H. Gundlach (Ed.), *Untersuchungen zur Geschichte der Psychologie und der Psychotechnik* (pp. 75–94). München-Wien: Profil.

Belzen, J. A. (2007). *Psychologie en het raadsel van de religie: Beschouwingen bij een eeuw godsdienstpsychologie in Nederland.* Amsterdam: Boom.

Belzen, J. A. (2015). *Religionspsychologie. Eine historische Analyse im Licht der Internationalen Gesellschaft* [Psychology of Religion. A Historical Analysis in the Light of Its International Association]. Berlin/Heidelberg (Germany): Springer.

Belzen, J. A. (2016). Criticisms, debates, and futures: The psychology of religion and its discontents. In W. B. Parsons (Ed.), *Religion: Social Religion* (pp. 85–102). Farmington Hills, MI (USA): Macmillan, 2016.

Bering, J. (2010). *The God instinct. The psychology of souls, destiny, and the meaning of life.* London: Nicholas Brealey.

Bresler, J. (1907). *Religionshygiene.* Halle a.d.S.: Marhold.

Dawkins, R. (2006). *The God delusion.* Boston: Houghton Mifflin.

Dennett, D. C. (2006). *Breaking the spell: Religion as a natural phenomenon.* New York: Penguin.

Dixon, S. L. (1999). *Augustine: The scattered and gathered self.* St. Louis, MO: Chalice Press.

Du Buy, J. (1904–1905). Stages of religious development. *American Journal of Religious Psychology and Education, 1,* 7–29.

Du Buy, J. (1908–1909). Four types of Protestants: A comparative study in the psychology of religion. *American Journal of Religious Psychology and Education, 3,* 165–209.

Faber, M. D. (2002). *The magic of prayer: An introduction to the psychology of faith.* Westport, CT/London: Praeger.

Faber, M. D. (2004). *The psychological roots of religious belief. Searching for angels and the parent-god.* Amherst, NY: Prometheus.

Faber, M. D. (2010). *Becoming God's children. Religion's infantilizing process.* Santa Barbara, CA (USA)/Oxford: Praeger.

Freud, S. (1907). Zwangshandlungen und Religionsübungen. *Zeitschrift für Religionspsychologie,* 1, 4–12.

Freud, S. (1913/1964). Totem and taboo. In *The standard edition of the complete psychological works of Sigmund Freud* (Vol. 13, pp. 1–161). London: Hogarth.

Freud, S. (1927/1961). The future of an illusion. In *The standard edition of the complete psychological works of Sigmund Freud* (Vol. 21, pp. 1–56). London: Hogarth.

Gleitman, H. (1985). Some trends in the study of cognition. In S. Koch & D. E. Leary (Eds.), *A century of psychology as science* (pp. 420–436). New York: McGraw Hill.

Hitchens, C. (2007). *God is not great: How religion poisons everything.* New York: Twelve Books.

Hood, R. W. (2001). *Dimensions of mystical experiences: Empirical studies and psychological links.* Amsterdam/New York: Rodopi.

Hood, R. W., & Williamson, W. P. (2008). *Them that believe: The power and meaning of the Christian serpent-handling tradition.* Berkeley: University of California Press.

Ideler, K. W. (1848). *Versuch einer Theorie des religiösen Wahnsinns: ein Beitrag zur Kritik der religiösen Wirren der Gegenwart.* 1. Teil: *Die Erscheinungen des religiösen Wahnsinns.* Halle: Schwetschke.

Ideler, K. W. (1850). *Versuch einer Theorie des religiösen Wahnsinns: ein Beitrag zur Kritik der religiösen Wirren der Gegenwart.* 2. Teil: *Die Entwickelung des religiösen Wahnsinns.* Halle: Schwetschke.

Koch, S., & Leary, D. E. (Eds.). (1985). *A century of psychology as science.* New York: McGraw Hill.

Kugelmann, R. (2011). *Psychology and Catholicism: Contested boundaries.* Cambridge/ New York: Cambridge University Press.

Jonte-Pace, D., & Parsons, W. B. (Eds.). (2001). *Religion and psychology: Mapping the terrain. Contemporary dialogues, future prospects.* London/New York: Routledge.

Malony, H. N. (2015). *Religion in the history of psychology.* (*Selected comments.*) Bloomington (IN, USA): XLibris.

Nauta, R. (2011). Review of Belzen, J. A. (2007) 'Psychologie en het raadsel van de religie: Beschouwingen bij een eeuw godsdienstpsychologie in Nederland'. *The International Journal for the Psychology of Religion, 21,* 77–80

Nørager, T. (1996). Metapsychology and discourse: A note on some neglected issues in the psychology of religion. *International Journal for the Psychology of Religion, 6,* 139–149.

Poloma, M. M., & Hood, R. W. (2008). *Blood and fire: Godly love in a Pentecostal emerging church.* New York/London: NYU Press.

Pargament, K. I. (2013). *APA-Handbook of psychology, religion and spirituality.* (Vols. 1–2) Washington, DC: American Psychological Association.

Parsons, W. B. (1999). *The enigma of the oceanic feeling: Revisioning the psychoanalytic theory of mysticism.* New York/Oxford: Oxford University Press.

Parsons, W. B. (2013). *Freud and Augustine in dialogue. Psychoanalysis, mysticism and the culture of modern spirituality.* Charlottesville/London: University of Virginia Press.

Pfister, O. (1905). Das Elend unserer wissenschaftlichen Glaubenslehre. *Schweizerische Theologische Zeitschrift, 22,* 209–212.

Resch, A. (1997). *Paranormologie und Religion.* Innsbruck: Resch Verlag.

Reuder, M. (1999). A history of Division 36 (Psychology of religion). In D. A. Dewsbury (Ed.), *Unification through division: Histories of the divisions of the APA* (Vol. IV, S. 91–108). Washington, DC: APA.

Reuterdahl, H. (1837). *Inledning till theologien* [Introduction to theology]. Lund: Gleerup.

Roscam Abbing, P. J. (1981). *Psychologie van de religie: Godsdienstpsychologie in verband met filosofie en theologie.* Assen: Van Gorcum.

Runze, G. (1894). *Die Psychologie des Unsterblichkeitsglaubens und der Unsterblichkeitsleugnung*. Berlin: Gaertner (Studien zur vergleichenden Religionswissenschaft, 2).

Scheler, M. (1912). Über Selbsttäuschungen. *Zeitschrift für Pathopsychologie, 1*, 87–163.

Scheler, M. (1913–1916/1921). *Der Formalismus in der Ethik und die materiale Wertethik* (2., unveränderte Auf.). Halle: Niemeyer.

Scheel, O. (1908). Die moderne Religionspsychologie. *Zeitschrift für Theologie und Kirche, 18*, 1–38.

Schleiermacher, F. D. E. (1799/1821). *Über die Religion: Reden an die Gebildeten unter ihren Verächtern*. Berlin: Reimer.

Stählin, W. (1968). *Via vitae: Lebenserinnerungen*. Kassel: Stauda.

Toomela, A., & Valsiner, J. (Eds.). (2010). *Methodological thinking in psychology: 60 years gone astray?* Charlotte, NC: Information Age.

Vergeer, C. (2008). Religie (2): Review of Belzen, J. A. (2007) 'Psychologie en het raadsel van de religie: Beschouwingen bij een eeuw godsdienstpsychologie in Nederland'. *Filosofie, 18*(1), 58–59.

Vergote, A. (1978/1988). *Guilt and desire: Religious attitudes and their pathological derivatives*. New Haven, CT: Yale University Press.

Vergote, A. (1983/1996). *Religion, belief and unbelief: Psychological study*. Amsterdam/Leuven: Rodopi/Leuven University Press.

Vergote, A. (1998). *'Tu aimeras le Seigneur ton Dieu'. L'identité chrétienne* [Thou shalt love the Lord thy God. The specificity of Christianity]. Paris: Cerf.

Vergote, A. (1999). *Moderniteit en Christendom. Gesprek in vrijheid en respect* [Modernity and Christianity. A conversation in freedom and respect]. Tielt: Lannoo.

Vergote, A. (2007). *Humanité de l'homme, divinité de Dieu* [The human being's humanity, God's divinity]. Paris: Cerf.

Vorbrodt, G. (1926). Arbeitsprogramm für zukünftige Religionspsychologie. *Religionspsychologie (Veröffentlichungen des Wiener Religionspsychologischen Forschungs-Institut), 1*, 91–98.

Westerink, H. (2012). *The heart of man's destiny. Lacanian psychoanalysis and early Reformation thought*. London/New York: Routledge.

Wundt, W. (1905). *Völkerpsychologie: Eine Untersuchung der Entwicklungsgesetze von Sprache, Mythos und Sitte*. Zweiter Band: *Mythos und Religion, erster Teil*. Leipzig: Engelmann.

Zimbardo, P. (2004). Does psychology make a significant difference in our lives? *American Psychologist, 59*, 339–351.

CHAPTER 2

A Very Short History of the International Association for the Psychology of Religion (Being at the Same Time a Quick Overview of Its Publication in *Religionspsychologie*)

Jacob A. Belzen

Summary

This chapter provides a very short history of the International Association for the Psychology of Religion by following the structure of a recent German book analyzing IAPR's past and international context.

As the centennial of both the *Archive for the Psychology of Religion* (ARP, original name: *Archiv für Religionspsychologie*) and the International Association for the Psychology of Religion (IAPR, original name: *Gesellschaft für Religionspsychologie*) was approaching, an extensive study of the history of this infrastructure for the field was undertaken. The report of this study is characterized by: 1) its empirical foundation (it is not a summary of "old" psychology of religion, but a piece of research based on primary sources, as kept in archives scattered in the main all over Europe); 2) its demythologizing and critical tendency (e.g., towards the myths about Oswald Külpe [1862–1915] as a psychologist of religion and about the so-called "Dorpat School" in the psychology of religion, and even towards the past work of the author himself); and 3) its effort to contextualize the results of the empirical research.

On behalf of those unable to read the report, in German, of the study of IAPR's contextualized history, the present text provides an overview of the structure and content (not a summary) of this report (Belzen, 2015).

The report is structured in three parts: an introduction (I), dealing with purpose, occasion, and method of the research, a middle part (II, chapters 2–10), centering on IAPR's history and its international context, and a final part (III, chapter 11), in which a number of "observations and notes" on "foundations, problems and perspectives" of the psychology of religion are articulated. Seven appendices list a number of external facts: nr. 1 on the main data in IAPR's

 | DOI 10.1163/9789004322011_003

history, nr. 2 lists its conferences, nr. 3 its presidents, nr. 4 the editors of *ARP*, nr. 5 relates the history of IAPR's awards and its predecessor (le Prix Quinquennial), nr. 6 lists the symposia of the European Group for the Psychology of Religion (1979–2003), and nr. 7 provides an overview of themes dealt with at these symposia. A list of abbreviations and archives is printed in the very beginning (pp. VII–VIII), a bibliography and a name index at the end.

Chapter 1 situates the research and it report within the discipline of the history of psychology (and some neighboring fields), discusses a number of (controversial) issues in the rare accounts of the history of the psychology of religion, and provides the rationale for the approach chosen. For reasons lined out (and resulting from the fact that IAPR as organization was completing its first century), the study focuses on organizational aspects of the psychology of religion, with theoretical reflection as an explicit horizon. Also in chapter 1, the structure of the main part (II) is explained: The five most important data in IAPR's first history have all been given a chapter, each but the last followed by a chapter in which developments in the broader international context within the psychology of religion are discussed. (Therefore, part II consists in 9 chapters.) It is announced that especially the earlier history, as most unknown, will be treated in detail; towards the end, chapters dealing with more recent developments tend to be much shorter.

Each of the chapters dealing with an important year in IAPR's history (1914, 1929, 1960, 2001, and 2015) provide an analysis of happenings in the psychology of religion and its international association preceding and leading up to the year in the chapter's title. So, the first historical chapter (chapter 2 of the book: "The Foundation – 1914") deals with developments in IAPR's prehistory, focusing, as announced, on organizational matters. Among other things, the direct forerunners of IAPR are discussed: the (first) German journal for the psychology of religion (*Zeitschrift für Religionspsychologie*, 1907–1913), to which Stanley Hall's *The American Journal of Religious Psychology (and Education)* probably served as an inspiration, the (German) Neurenberg Working Group for the Psychology of Religion (*religionspsychologische Arbeitsgemeinschaft*), and *ARP*, on behalf of which IAPR was founded as a supporting organization.

Chapter 3 ("Fighting About the Psychology of Religion") takes a look at the context in especially the German speaking European countries, as relevant to the (pre)history of IAPR and *ARP*. It was a history full of expectations towards, but also struggles and outright fights about the psychology of religion, its nature, its approaches, etc. The role of Wilhelm Stählin (1883–1975), founder of both *ARP* and IAPR (and previously active in the *Zeitschrift für Religionspsychologie* and the *arbeitspsychologische Arbeitsgemeinschaft* is analyzed.

Chapter 4 ("The Second Beginning – 1929") introduces shortly the first members of the board of the 1914 founded Association for the Psychology of Religion and their first activities. The disastrous consequences of World War I for IAPR are related: What had begun so fiercely was destroyed almost completely (all that remained apparently being some occasional correspondence between some members of the board; Stählin managed only 1921 to finally publish *ARP* no. 2/3, the printing of which had been almost finished in 1914 already). In 1927, Werner Gruehn (1887–1961), a pastor from Estonia, turned to Stählin as he wanted to continue the interests of his teacher Karl Girgensohn (1875–1925) in the psychology of religion and in the infrastructure founded on its behalf. He became the next editor of *ARP* and Secretary-General of IAPR, publishing *ARP* no. 4 in 1929.

Chapter 5 ("Fiercest Fighting in the Psychology of Religion") deals with some other international initiatives that elsewhere had been taken on behalf of the psychology of religion, especially with the work of Karl Beth (1872–1959) and Marianne Beth (born Weisl, 1890–1984). Since 1922 they had organized meetings on the psychology of religion in their home in Vienna (where German Karl had become a professor of theology). In 1924 they formally founded an international association for the psychology of religion, as organizational context for a "research institute for the psychology of religion", since 1926 publishing a "journal for the psychology of religion" (*Zeitschrift für Religionspsychologie*). The chapter analyses the context and inspirations of their activities and describes what remains perhaps the largest meeting ever organized for the psychology of religion solely: the "First International Congress for the Psychology of Religion" in Vienna (May 26–31, 1931). As by the end of the 1920s also Gruehn started to revive IAPR and ARP, he considered the activities of the Beth-couple as important rivals that needed to be combated. (In the course of the rivalry with Beth, Gruehn began adding "international" to IAPR's initial name.) Despite efforts of some persons on both Beth's and IAPR's part to work towards integration and/or reconciliation, a veritable fight between the two organizations (or rather: between Gruehn and Beth) was the result. (Gruehn explicitly employing the term "fiercest fight".) The end of it all was again caused by political constellations leading to another World War: Gruehn became increasingly involved with National-Socialism (and apparently lost his interest in IAPR and *ARP*) and the Beths (Marianne being Jewish) were forced into exile. Both journals for the psychology of religion ceased publication well before WWII.

Chapter 6 ("The Reconstitution – 1960") deals in greater detail with activities by Gruehn, sometimes named "psychology of religion" but oftentimes hardly related to this subject. It also recounts IAPR's only conference held before WWII: in Erfurt (Germany), June 27–29, 1930. Only after WWII Gruehn, who had fled Berlin (where he had been appointed a full professor of theology in 1937) fearing the Communist invasion, took up his correspondence as "General-Secretary" again. Isolated, lonely and ill, he tried from Hanover, where he served his church for some time, to revive IAPR and to organize a "second international congress for the psychology" by the end of the 1950s (it never came about, however). Although in fact, nothing had remained of both IAPR and *ARP*, he managed to correspond with politicians, applying for funding, and with a number of persons from IAPR's past. He came into contact with Wilhelm Keilbach (1908–1982), a Roman Catholic priest from Serbia, like Gruehn belonging to a German minority. He had dealt with Girgensohn's work in his doctoral dissertation (defended in Rom) and had been appointed professor of theology in Munich (Germany). He became Gruehn's successor as Secretary-General of IAPR, at that time an organization existing on paper only. He organized a small-scale conference (*Tagung*) in 1960 (attended essentially by a very small number of people who had been acquainted with IAPR before WWII), at which IAPR was formerly "reconstituted".

Chapter 7 ("On International Congresses in the Psychology of Religion, 1900–1960") deals again with a number of other organizations in the psychology of religion and discusses especially some of the "international" conferences they organized (or intended to organize). Next to Beth's conference in Vienna, the sessions on psychology within the International Congresses for Psychology are discussed (leading to what may have been the first conference on solely this subject in 1926, in Utrecht, the Netherlands) as well as the conference announced for 1959 by a Swiss organization founded by Willy Canziani (1933–2013), a Swiss psychologist (who had also studied theology). Keilbach suggested Canziani to leave the organizational field to IAPR, being in the process of reconstitution, and invited him to join its board. Also, the difficulties surrounding Gruehn's never realized second congress are related and the problems Keilbach (joined again by Stählin) had in dealing with Gruehn during his last years.

Chapter 8 ("The Reorganization – 2001") briefly relates the few things that happened within IAPR after its reconstitution in 1960. Keilbach initially had become quite active: He managed to publish a volume of ARP again (the next ones followed very irregularly, with sometimes up to four years between them) and funded by the German government he travelled extensively in order to establish relationships in quite a number of countries. Although he had been successful in attracting new attendants of the conferences and authors for the ARP (among them well-known persons like Antoon Vergote, André Godin, Benjamin Beit-Hallahmi, and Hjalmar Sundén), the pace rapidly slowed down. Especially after Keilbach's death, an increasing gap to developments in academic psychology, theology and religious studies became apparent. By the end of the 20th century, IAPR was almost non-existing again. In 2001, IAPR needed to be founded a fourth time.

Chapter 9 ("The Comeback of [also of Quarreling in] the Psychology of Religion") relates a number of organizational initiatives in IAPR's international context, especially such that have been of some influence within IAPR. Among the infrastructure dealt with are the Society for the Scientific Study of Religion and its flagship, the prestigious *Journal for the Scientific Study of Religion* (JSSR), the Division 36 of the American Psychological Association (APA), *The International Journal for the Psychology of Religion* (IJPR), Lumen Vitae (where André Godin was based) and the establishment of full professorships for the psychology of religion in a number of European countries (notably among them: The Netherlands, Belgium, and Sweden). Special attention is given to an informal, but quite influential network in European psychology of religion at the end of the 20th century: In clear opposition to IAPR, the "European Psychologists of Religion" (EPR) was the result of dissatisfaction among younger Dutch and Scandinavian attendants of IAPR's 1977 conference in Uppsala (Sweden). They gathered a number of times in Nijmegen (The Netherlands) and in a number of other cities all over Europe, attracted an increasing number of people and established relationships with other infrastructure as established since the 1960s. As there was an interest to "save" the "old" infrastructure (IAPR), a good number of participants in EPR attended IAPR's 2001-conference, joining and voting in favor of a reorganization. In fact, ERP had taken over IAPR. On the co-sponsored 2003-conference in Glasgow (Scotland, UK), EPR abolished itself, leaving the field, organizationally, to IAPR.

Chapter 10 ("A Century Completed – 2015") relates in just a few pages the main happenings within IAPR since its last founding, to which belong the transformation of *ARP* into a regularly published journal.

After these nine historical chapters on IAPR, part III (identical with chapter 11) of the book *Religionspsychologie* consists in nine paragraphs of an essayistic nature: From a meta-perspective a number of issues pertaining to the psychology of religion are being discussed, their overarching characterization being "plurality" (*Pluriformität*). They deal with the plural relationships between religion and psychology (of which psychology of religion is only one) (§1), the plural object of the psychology of religion (§2), the plural attitudes towards religion found in this field (§3), its plural foundations (§4), contexts (§5) and conditions for origin and growth (§6), the plural types of progress in (§7) and the plural benefits of the psychology of religion (§8), closing with some words on this plural enterprise on its way into the future (§9). A few of the notes and observations from this last chapter have turned up in the introductory essay to the present volume.

References

Belzen, J. A. (2015). *Religionspsychologie. Eine historische Analyse im Licht der Internationalen Gesellschaft* [Psychology of Religion. A Historical Analysis in the Light of Its International Association]. Berlin/Heidelberg (Germany): Springer.

CHAPTER 3

More Than One Psychology of Religion in the House of the International Association for the Psychology of Religion

Jozef Corveleyn

Summary

In his minutely constructed book on the history of psychology of religion, Belzen pays correct attention to the organizational and methodological contributions of Antoine Vergote in the course of the last half of this century long history. In this short article, the author highlights a few aspects of Vergote's intellectual approach in the psychology of religion that inevitably remain underexposed in Belzen's already long book. First focus is the background of Vergote's plea for a strict neutrality, be it with interest, and thus benevolent, as the basic attitude of the researcher in this domain. Despite this plea, it is quite clear how much his own approach was influenced by his personal reading of Christianism. Second, the author focuses the "Latin" (French) sources of inspiration in the work of Vergote. And he hypothesizes that this probably is the reason for the lack of a widespread influence of his work in the international world of the psychology of religion.

Introduction

Minutely constructed with a nearly loving attention for its object, the psychology of religion, this latest book of Jacob Belzen is a gem or a treasure for the actual and the future study of that domain, as well as of the adjacent domains of practical or pastoral theology, the philosophy of religion, and of religious studies in general. Because, like all excellent historical works on *Ideeengeschichte* (history of ideas), the work of Belzen is not only a detailed, narrative report on the course of the history of the discipline in the overall context of the history of psychology in general, it is at the same time a well-thought reflection about and an interrogation of the content and the limits of this sub-discipline of psychology.

During the last four decades (e.g., see Belzen, 2007, 2009, 2012) he has not only observed and documented the sometimes very complicated evolution

 | DOI 10.1163/9789004322011_004

and growth of this part of psychology, he has been a very active participant of, and an active player in the field of our domain (Belzen, 1997, 2010; Hood & Belzen, 2013). His book can thus be described as the recount of a participative observer, at least of the second half of the century of the history of the psychology of religion until today.

One of his participative activities has been and is the building of bridges. Bridges between scientific disciplines (psychology, theology, philosophy, history), between tendencies in the discipline (think of the methodology debate in psychology, the question of limits in the definition of the object of the psychology of religion), between Europe and North America, and between schools and traditions in the psychology of religion, as well as in the different Christian denominations.

As far as I know the recent history of our domain, Belzen was and is excellently positioned to perform this building of bridges. And moreover, he used this position actively. His already long scholarly life has not only completely been devoted to the study of the many meanders of mainstream psychology of religion, he never has been afraid of discovering new perspectives, other cultural environments and other traditions than his own (Dutch) tradition, which is very much influenced by Anglo-Saxon, German, and Scandinavian tendencies. Very early in his career his attention has been drawn to the South. He made great efforts to overcome barriers of language and of mentality and so, he marched into the French and Italian approach of the psychology of religion, which leaded him to Brussels, Leuven, and Louvain-la-Neuve in Belgium and to Paris in France and to the University of Milano in Italy.

The Latin Approach of the Psychology of Religion

In this contribution, I want to focus this interest of Belzen and his efforts to integrate this "Latin" approach of the psychology of religion into the mainstream by favoring the dialogue and mutual understanding. All of this is paradigmatically illustrated by his approach in the actual book of the work of Antoine Vergote. Belzen knew very well the master and his works. And although he pays appropriate attention to the role of this historical figure in the history of the (mainly European) psychology of religion, some content-related aspects and some characteristics of his contribution remain, inevitably, underexposed. The standpoint of Antoine Vergote concerning the definition of the psychology of religion comes clearly into the fore in Belzen's reports about Vergote's role in the history of the reorganization of the IAPR since the sixties (chapter 8) as well as in the evolution of the European group (chapter 9), founded in

1979 in the Nijmeghen meetings. Not taking the lead in these organizational matters, as Belzen clearly demonstrates, Vergote was nevertheless always devoted to the "cause", the promotion of a "real" psychology of religion, i.e., a psychology that is independent of one's own religious conviction, as well as of institutionalized religion; a psychology that is focusing religion as socio-cultural phenomenon that impregnates or can impregnate the individual psyche, not a psychology in the service of religion, neither a "religion" that is mainly considered as a personal emotional state. I will highlight in what follows, some of the backgrounds of this outspoken standpoint that he maintained until his last intervention at the IAPR congress in Bari (2011).

This definition-question invites us to go back to two important topics. First, the basic elements of his scientific convictions and some of the sources of inspiration for his specific approach to the psychology of religion. Second, there is the unavoidable value- and idea- ladenness of his approach to religion and to the psychology of religion, as is unavoidably the case in every psychology(-ist) of religion.

Methodological Neutrality and Value-Ladenness

To begin with the second point. Belzen very correctly underlines that it was typical for Vergote's approach that he "opposed against each amalgamation of religion and psychology" (Belzen, 2015, p. 171). Indeed, in every discussion about the definition of psychology of religion and of the specific object of this branch of psychology, namely the "religion", Vergote advocated a strict delimitation between psychology and religion. He pleaded for a strictly neutral approach to religion by the human scientist, psychologist or sociologist, historian or cultural anthropologist. The scientist must adhere to a strict "abstinence of an ontological judgment" about the "object" of religious belief, the "god"-figure. In his latest "handbook" (1984) as in the earlier version (1966) or at other occasions, Vergote states:

> As an empirical science psychology of religion directs itself to the examination of observable phenomena. These are explained, in part, by placing them in the context of the functioning of the subjective life. They are thus not observed in the light of an ontology, nor are they interpreted according to theological principles. Religious psychology is not competent to make pronouncements concerning the reality or the properties of the supernatural to which religion refers [This is what Théodore Flournoy[1]

1 1845–1920; Professor in psychology at Geneva University.

> called] the "methodological exclusion of the transcendent". (Vergote, 1997, p. 27)

This statement has two logical consequences. The first is that psychology "neither can prove nor discount specific religious propositions". And, somehow provocatively: "Statements such as 'God exists' or 'Christ is risen' make no sense, psychologically speaking" (Vergote, 1997). The second consequence is that the psychologist never can do appeal, in his pursuit of explanation, to the supernatural as an explanatory element. Referring to concrete beliefs (the belief in the Holy Spirit of God, the resurrection of Christ, etc.) and to religious practices (prayer and rituals), Vergote states:

> Psychology can observe these beliefs and must take them into account because they are also psychological data. In view of the specifically religious character of their meanings these statements of faith make no sense within the scientific context for they are not susceptible to empirical verification or falsification. (Vergote, 1997, p. 28)

Although he did hold himself always very strictly to these principles of neutrality and "ontological abstinence", in all his reports on empirical psychological researches (e.g., Vergote & Tamayo, 1980) he has conducted, as well as in his strict psychological writings, his sympathy for and his involvement in "his" (Catholic) Christian belief nevertheless transpires in many texts and at different occasions. It is not so that he ever apologetically defended "his" religion, nor that he explicitly tried to demonstrate the great or superior value of "his" belief. But, it *transpires* in this psychological writings, and, of course, he writes *openly* about his belief in other writings and surely in his more theological and personal testimonial writings, written after his career as a psychological researcher.

That it resounds can shortly be made clear by referring, for example, to his obvious sympathy for the love mysticism of Theresa of Avila (see Vergote, 1978/1988) as an example of a not-pathological extreme form of passionate love of a Christian for her God. This being at home in the Christian world of belief and his sympathy for it, is also reflected in the starting point of this book on *Guilt and Desire*. From the start, he takes position, undoubtedly a Christian position. In this book he wants to demonstrate, so he states, that there are two basic anthropological dimensions in Christianity. And that this can be "objectively" demonstrated via psycho(-patho)logical and psychoanalytic data and analyses of "facts". Without any preceding nor following argumentation, he states this even more broadly, already in the third paragraph of the 'preface': "Debt and desire represent two basic dimensions of existence. For this reason, these two themes are at the heart of both religion and psychoanalysis" (Vergote, 1978/1988, p. viii). It is not explained where he takes this from, or on what cultural, historical, or philosophical analysis this assertion is based. And this statement is not about Christianity, no, it is about "religion and psychoanalysis", in general thus. Of course in this statement all kinds of references are echoed from the history of philosophy and theology. But, it is a statement, to be taken for granted, so it seems. One can imagine other possible analyses for defining the "essential dimensions" of "existence", or of "religion" and "psychoanalysis". William James (1902), for example, focused the emotional experience of the believer, in his analysis of the psychological essentials of religious belief and how it impacts on human live. This is a particular perspective determined by a Christian tradition of philosophy (subjectivity in the center of understanding human belief), but he too was speaking about "varieties of [the] religious experience".

More than one question could be raised here. I will point to two topics. The first topic is the question why Vergote states his axiomatic definition from the start of this mainly clinical research book, which is the *Guilt and Desire* book. From where, or based on which argumentation does the accentuation of these affective-motivational dimensions in "religion" stem from? The second topic is the question whether this taking a stand from the start of a research endeavor is scientifically permitted or, simply unavoidable.

To the first topic it can be said that, undoubtedly, when Vergote in his 1978 book is speaking of "religion", he is doing this from his Catholic, then contemporaneous interpretation of Christianity. Of course, he wants to say something fundamental in this book about this universal human cultural phenomenon, namely religion, but, without being apologetic, he (unavoidably) takes the perspective of his own cultural background and personal belief interpretation. This book is clearly not about "religion" or religious belief in general, but about a particular approach and interpretation of Christian experience, illuminated with the particularities of the human sciences approach of the time in which it has been written, influenced by phenomenological philosophical anthropology and by the contemporaneous dominant psychoanalytic approach on the European continent.

After his career as a psychoanalyst and as a psychology researcher, he was very open about the basic dimensions of his personal belief as an active Christian, in a pair of theological books (Vergote, 1997/1998, 2006). The first mentioned of these is, for his normal way of doing, very personal, so to speak confessing, and self-revelatory. He demonstrates how central and important he considers the personal relationship of the human being with God in the person of Jesus in "the" (his) experience of Christian belief. He speaks prudently of "in my opinion", but it is his central conviction (and experience). What is central in this relationship? Right, *guilt and desire*. The title of the book is a quote from the New Testament (Mt. 22:34–40; Mk. 12, 28–31): "You shall love the Lord your God ...". And this commandment of loving of the Lord comprises for him also this other incitement of Jesus, in the same line as the just quoted, namely "love your enemies", expressed in: "Therefore you are to be perfect, as your heavenly Father is perfect" (Mt. 5:48), preceded by "If you greet only your brothers, what more are you doing than others? Do not even the Gentiles do the same?" (Mt. 5:47). Guilt is linked to this exhortation toward perfection. In reference to this exhortation, he introduces the "guilt" dimension in his *Guilt and Desire* book (Vergote 1978/1988, p. 43 ff, p. 78). Guilt has, in his reading as a philosopher and as a psychoanalyst, a twofold significance: guilt as a basic dimension of the human existential condition: the standing in debt towards God on one side (personal existence as a gift) and guilt as the unavoidable feeling that accompanies the experience of our shortcomings in regard to the fundamental exhortation (and the herewith related desire for) toward perfection.

The scientific psychological and psychoanalytic analysis of the basic dimensions of "the religion" and "human existence" is thus from the beginning implicitly based on a theological interpretation of "a" religious tradition and on the personal experience of a personal belief system. Is this personal touch in scientific research in a human science like psychology, simply unavoidable because a partly interpretative science cannot be practiced "*in abstracto*" or "de-humanized", or is this nevertheless an illicit or a questionable way (even if it is unconsciously done) to promote a particular belief system to the status of "standard" for "the" religion? Difficult to say in this case. It can be that Vergote considered "his" Christendom as the culmination point of the evolution of the monotheistic religions-of-the-book, refined as it is, in his opinion, by centuries of history (see Vergote, 2006). But it is difficult to prove that this stand, most probably based on his theological analysis and personal belief, prevailed in or determined his composition of the *Guilt and Desire* book. But even, if it were so, the question can be raised if this taking of a standpoint in this kind of qualitative-empirically based compositions is unavoidable, even if it is questionable? Or should this kind of analyses be simply judged as illicit and thus as simply unscientific, because it is standpoint-based? I believe this is not a simple either-or matter. As it is stated in handbooks of qualitative research like the magnificent one, edited by Denzin and Lincoln (2000) for example, the value- and idea-ladenness of science is unavoidable because it is intrinsic to all scientific research. The only measure one can take is to make the standpoint transparent and to openly discuss it. In the introductory section of his *Guilt and Desire* book, Vergote regularly shows his cards, i.e., his sources of inspiration in theology, philosophy, medical psychology and psychoanalysis, but nowhere he gives opening to his personal convictions and beliefs, as they are based in these sources of inspiration. This can be regretted afterwards; more openness about his personal standpoint and visions could have helped to more open discussions about his findings reported in the book and about the broader applicability of them, in other cultural spheres than only in the Christian "world". Perhaps it is for this reason that this book and also other components of his contribution to the psychology of religion have received not more resonance in the international community of this branch of psychology than they deserve on the basis of the intellectual qualities inherent to these works. This limited resonance is illustrated in Belzen's actual book: The standpoints of Vergote were very much respected and he has had a "tangible" influence in the growing organization of the psychology of religion, mainly in Europe, but he could not launch an intellectual "school" of broadly academically accepted empirical psychology of religion, inspired by his wide and widening intellectual insights – psychological theory, philosophical anthropology, theology, cultural anthropology and psychoanalysis – in the phenomenon of religion and religious behavior.

Maybe this somehow surprising lack of impact, is also partly due to the "Latin" (say French) origin of his main sources of intellectual inspiration in the field of human sciences.

Sources of Inspiration for "His" Psychology of Religion

Although he did not neglect the contributions of internationally influential authors in the Anglo-Saxon communities of psychology and philosophy, his most important references were the continental philosophers on one side and the then – also internationally – still leading French human scientists. This *avant-garde* leadership of the French human sciences lasted until the eighties of last century, and, was not really recognized in the North-American academic world, except perhaps in some schools of philosophy and of comparative literature. In no way it was really influential in academic psychology.

When I say that he did not neglect the internationally recognized contributions coming from the Anglo-Saxon world, I am referring to Vergote's due attention – not *per se* his agreement with – to authors like Gordon Allport and his school on personality research, Henry Murray and his work on projective tests, Abraham Maslow's motivational theory, Erik Erikson's (although born in Germany, he nevertheless can be considered an American psychologist) developmental view on becoming religiously believing and James Fowler's research on the stages of faith development. In the domain of philosophy he only paid attention to the British analytic philosophy of language.

When Vergote was commissioned, at the end of the fifties of last century, to start the new chair of the psychology of religion at the University of Leuven, he went to the, at that time, *mecca* of the humanities, namely the University of Paris, and the High Schools in the same city. This is very well reported in Belzen's book (see Belzen, 2015, pp. 171, ff.), where he enumerates all the teachings Vergote took in the fields of philosophy, psychoanalysis, psychology, cultural anthropology, linguistics and sociology, all relevant in his view for the foundation of a true and well-reflected "psychology" of religion. The impact of this long-term intellectual immersion on his views on psychology in general and on the psychology of religion in particular, cannot be underestimated. It is not really focused in Belzen's historical analysis, except perhaps for the explanation of Vergote's continuous opposition against the "the mixing of religion and psychology" (Belzen, 2015).

It is not my ambition to make here, in the limited space of an article, a quick "deconstruction-reconstruction" of Vergote's intellectual baggage as a psychologist of religion. Others have done that in recent times (see e.g., Lecuit, 2007; Olemans, 2012, 2015). The main names have been mentioned in Belzen (2015). Here, I will limit myself to bring into the fore, three characteristic dimensions of Vergote's particular approach to the psychology of religion which most probably have become also the stumbling blocks for many of his colleagues in Europe and elsewhere, and for the later generations of psychologists of religion, to enter into a real dialogue with his views and to really integrate parts of his perspective into their currently ongoing research.

First of all, there is his view on the necessary interdisciplinarity of the psychology of religion. For him, the personal belief of an individual or her/his "religiosity" are the "result" of an ongoing *interaction* between, what can be called after Hegel, the objective religion (religion as a socio-cultural *fact*) on the one hand, and the personal (psycho)dynamics on the other. If psychology is the scientific study of this 'result', it cannot be practiced in isolation from the other human sciences (see Vergote, 1966, 1983/1997, 1988). The phenomenon of personal religiosity is thus so complex that one human science apart is not capable to fully understand or make understandable the entirety of this phenomenon. To put it in another way: religion, nor religiosity can be explained "away" by psychology on itself. This is the basis of his permanent opposition towards Freud's reductionist approach to religion in *The Future of an Illusion* (Freud, 1927). Religion is a universal component of each and every human community. It is formed by ages of history in a particular geographically situated social environment The psychologist cannot neglect these contexts, even when studying the "behaviors" of today-participants to well-designed empirical researches. He/she must contextualize his current observations in the required historical, theological, linguistic, sociological, and philosophical perspectives. And most of the time, if not always, Vergote practices this interdisciplinarity in his comments on empirical findings of psychology of religion (see Vergote & Tamayo, 1980). Or, he most of the time presents the empirical psychological findings in a very contextualized paper or chapter. This is very tangible in almost all of the chapters in his so-called handbooks on psychology of religion (Vergote, 1966, 1983/1997) when speaking of emotions, motivations, cognitive development, etc., in the realm of religious "behavior". This makes the study of many of his texts so difficult and complicated. Complicated, but also relevant to and in conformity with the complexity of the phenomenon under study (see also Hood & Belzen, 2013).

What Vergote typically brought home from his exploration of the humanities in Paris in the fifties and sixties, was the structuralist view on human existence. Although he was not entirely agreeing with the "disappearance" of the subject and the de-constructionist vision on human reality as propagated by Michel Foucault or Jacques Derrida (see his vision on psychoanalysis and Lacan in Vergote & Moyaert, 1988), he nevertheless always underlines in his studies of religious behavior, the non-subjective component in it. The human individual, the individual believer is part of a socio-cultural system or structure. He/she "receives" the religion to which she adheres, the god he believes in, the ritual to which she is participating. Religious belief is not my personal creation, nor my most-individual "feeling". It is my way of integrating what I am told by others. And, all of this, is told to me in many ways, but, it is given to me, not invented by me, not my creation. It is a gift that comes to me, essentially by the language I am speaking after having received it from my immediate environment in the family, part of a larger community, with its own history, its own stories, texts, and *codices*.

What possibly hinders a lot of contemporaneous psychologists of religion (his generation and the next generations of academic psychologists) is Vergote's continuous quasi-exegetical referrencing to the classical Freud texts. Although he is not a blind and obedient "follower" of Freud, it cannot be denied that he is in continuous discussion with the historical master. As Dirk Olemans (2012, 2015) very well demonstrates, Vergote's psychology of religion is very much influenced by his reading and interpretation of Freud's vision on the human psyche and has come into being in a continuous dialogue and discussion with Freud's views on religion and religiosity. This makes his psychology of religion very idiosyncratic and for the non-psychodynamically-trained academic psychologist sometimes inaccessible, if not entirely objectionable because of its constant reference to the, for the psychological *academia*, reprehensible psychoanalysis.

References

Belzen, J. A. (Ed.). (1997). *Hermeneutical approaches in psychology of religion*. Amsterdam/ Atlanta: Rodopi.

Belzen, J. A. (2007). *Psychologie en het raadsel van de religie: Beschouwingen bij een eeuw godsdienstpsychologie in Nederland*. Amsterdam: Boom.

Belzen, J. A. (2009). *Changing the scientific study of religion: Beyond Freud? Theoretical, empirical and clinical studies from psychoanalytic perspectives*. Dordrecht/Heidelberg/ London/New York: Springer.

Belzen, J. A. (2010). *Towards cultural psychology of religion. Principles, approaches, applications*. Dordrecht/Heidelberg/London/New York: Springer.

Belzen, J. A. (Ed.). (2012). *Psychology of religion: Autobiographical accounts*. New York: Springer.

Belzen, J. A. (2015). *Religionspsychologie. Eine historische Analyse im Spiegel der internationalen Gesellschaft*. Berlin und Heidelberg: Springer Verlag.

Denzin, N. K., & Lincoln, Y. S. (Eds.). (2000). *Handbook of qualitative research* (2nd ed.). Thousand Oaks, CA, London, New Delhi: Sage Publications.

Hood, R. W., & Belzen, J. A. (2013). Research methods in the psychology of religion and spirituality. In R. F. Paloutzian & C. L. Park (Eds.), *Handbook of the psychology of religion and spirituality* (2nd ed., pp. 75–93). New York: The Guilford Press.

James, W. (1902). *The varieties of religious experience: A study in human nature*. The Gifford Lectures on Natural Religion Delivered at Edinburgh in 1901–1902. London/ Bombay: Longmans, Green, & Co.

Lecuit, J.-B. (2007). *L'anthropologie théologique à la lumière de la psychanalyse. La contribution majeure d'Antoine Vergote*. Paris: Cerf.

Olemans, D. (2012). Theologie en psychoanalyse in het oeuvre van Antoon Vergote. *Bijdragen. International Journal in Philosophy and Theology, 73*, 55–84.

Olemans, D. (2015). *Psychoanalyse in Vergotes godsdienstpsychologie: Een grondslagenonderzoek* (Doctoral dissertation in Psychology). Leuven: KU Leuven. Retrieved from: <https://www.kuleuven.be/research/researchdatabase/project/3H09/3H090423.htm>.

Vergote, A. (1959). Le symbole. *Revue philosophique de Louvain, 57*, 197–224.

Vergote, A. (1966). *Psychologie religieuse*. Bruxelles: Dessart.

Vergote, A. (1970). *Religionspsychologie*. Olten/Freiburg im Breisgau: Walter-Verlag.

Vergote, A. (1978/1988). *Dette et désir. Deux axes chrétiens et la dérive pathologique.* Paris: Editions du Seuil [English version: *Guilt and Desire : Religious attitudes and their pathological derivatives* (M. H. Wood, Trans.)]. New Haven and London: Yale University Press.

Vergote, A. (1983/1997). Religion, foi, incroyance. Étude psychologique. Liège: Mardaga [In English: *Religion, belief and unbelief: A psychological study*]. Leuven/Amsterdam-Atlanta, GA: Leuven University Press and Rodopi.

Vergote, A. (1997). *La psychanalyse à l'épreuve de la sublimation.* Paris: Les Editions du Cerf.

Vergote, A. (1997/1998). *"De Heer je God liefhebben": het eigene van het Christendom.* Tielt: Uitgeverij Lannoo nv. Uit het Frans vertaald door Paul Leemans. (oorspronkelijk: « Tu aimeras le Seigneur ton Dieu ... ». L'identité chrétienne, Paris, Cerf – Montréal, Médiaspaul, 1997).

Vergote, A. (2006). *Humanité de l'homme, divinité de Dieu.* Paris: Éd. du Cerf

Vergote, A. (2011). *La psychanalyse devant la schizophrénie.* Paris: Les Editions du Cerf.

Vergote, A., & Moyaert, P. (Eds.). (1988). *Psychoanalyse. De mens en zijn lotgevallen.* Kapellen: De Nederlandsche Boekhandel/Uitgeverij Pelckmans.

Vergote, A., & Tamayo A. (1980). *The parental figures and the representation of God: A psychological and cross-cultural study.* The Hague/Paris/New York: Mouton Publishers and Leuven, Leuven University Press.

CHAPTER 4

Psychology of Religion: *Semper Militans*

Nils G. Holm

Summary

Studying the history of psychology of religion, especially through the *Internationale Gesellschaft für Religionspsychologie* (IAPR), one is struck by the many problems and conflicts there have been. Not only have world wars had their negative influence, but also personal controversies. Drawing on his personal experience, the author illustrates some of these. There are also problems on a more fundamental level, however: psychology of religion usually studies phenomena that are often interpreted on a supernatural level, as God's intervention. Conflicts between religious and psychological, more mundane interpretations therefore often occur. Drawing on his empirical research on glossolalia, the author makes a plea for peaceful co-existence of different interpretations. He concludes that psychology of religion is *semper militans*.

The psychology of religion originated in two key scientific disciplines that emerged in the 19th century. One is the general history of religion, which grew considerably in popularity in the late 1800s in countries such as Germany, France, and the Netherlands. The other discipline is general psychology, which at roughly the same time detached itself from philosophy to form an independent scientific field. From an early stage of the new discipline of psychology, religion was an interesting research object. This is obvious primarily in the work of the well-known American researchers in the field: G. Stanley Hall, E. D. Starbuck, and James H. Leuba. However, the most famous of all American pioneers within the psychology of religion is William James, who wrote the much appreciated and used work *The Varieties of Religious Experience* (1902). There were early researchers in the psychology of religion also in Europe. I will here mention Wilhelm Wundt, W. Stählin, Karl Girgensohn, and Werner Grühn. In addition to these, there are researchers in depth psychology, the main ones being, of course, Sigmund Freud and C. G. Jung.

Conflicts arose within the discipline at an early stage. These were not only due to the differences between depth psychology and the more psycho-physiological approach. Aspects contributing to the conflict also included personality clashes, and the question of whether religion could be studied

 | DOI 10.1163/9789004322011_005

psychologically at all. The divergence between theology and psychology has frequently been the background to the dissension. The two great wars in Europe have also had a dramatic impact on the development of the psychology of religion.

Much of this development can be read about in surveys that have been written on the emergence of the psychology of religion. For those able to read Finnish, there is an excellent work by Matti Luoma on the development of the psychology of religion in Europe and the USA: *Uskonnonpsykologia eilen ja tänään* ("The Psychology of Religion Yesterday and Today"), published in 1965. Another more recent overview is one in German by Jacob A. Belzen (2015), *Religionspsychologie. Eine historische Analyse im Spiegel der Internationalen Gesellschaft* ("The Psychology of Religion. The History of Its International Association"). The latter work is extensive, without being totally exhaustive. It gives us a thorough presentation of the beginnings of the psychology of religion, mainly in Europe, and the various events surrounding the establishment of the *Internationale Gesellschaft für Religionspsychologie* ("International Association for Psychology of Religion") in 1914. The book also provides an analysis and survey of developments up to the present day. The book, in my opinion, is a very valuable resource for anybody wishing to explore issues concerning the psychological study of religion. The final chapter, on the basic questions of what religion is and what the psychology of religion might contribute to the understanding of religion, are of particular interest. My brief reflections, presented below, are actually comments on some of Belzen's analyses. Other overviews with information on the emergence of the psychology of religion both in the USA and Europe are found in, for example, David Wulff's *Psychology of Religion. Classic and Contemporary Views* (1991).

A feature apparent in the presentations of these books is the many conflicts within the field. Here, I do not take into consideration purely personal antagonisms, but wish to somewhat illuminate the more fundamental issues involved in the scientific and psychological study of religion.

At a very early stage, a central question was whether it was feasible for a scholar to study religion without being religious him or herself, or at least without having had a personal experience of religiosity. This was discussed at one of the first conferences of psychology in Geneva in 1909. Attitudes expressed here included the assertion that an experience of conversion, in the religious sense, was as important for the psychologist of religion as the test tube was for the chemist. However, this assertion was not upheld, as a majority of the participants agreed with the finding that a scholar possesses a sufficient power of insight as a human being to be able to conduct research on religion. That one does not need to be criminal oneself in order to study criminal individuals was an argument presented by Leuba, among others. This has since been the standard and prevailing stance in the field of research into religion.

My personal experiences of the organisational circumstances within the psychology of religion go back to 1977, when the *Internationale Gesellschaft für Religionspsychologie* held a conference in Uppsala, Sweden. This was a very interesting experience for me. I gave my paper in German and talked about my research into glossolalia, which at that point was a very new research area. It was obvious that there was a rift between those who preferred speaking in German and those who preferred English. Most of the German-speakers had a background in theology, mainly Catholic fundamental theology. The English-speakers wanted to introduce more modern research approaches, more closely related to general psychology.

The divergences between the two groups were so strong that the younger, and mostly English-speaking, scholars wanted to break away, and they therefore established a parallel group for psychologists of religion, which started to convene every third year. The conflicts between the two groups were at times quite conspicuous. Personally, I was active within both of these groups. I was elected vice chair for the *Gesellschaft* in 1984 and later became its chair. I was also given the responsibility for the publication *Archiv für Religionspsychologie* ("Archive for the Psychology of Religion"). My dedicated goal was to ensure that the older association, established in 1914, would not disappear entirely, but would be able to merge with the newer group. Important was that the publication of the older organisation could be continued. There were, however, several problems.

In 1999, a crunch point was reached on the board of the *Gesellschaft*. Having discussed changes in the regulations and other matters, the issue of the location for the next conference was on the agenda. One suggestion was Eichstätt in Germany and another Soesterberg in the Netherlands. Obviously, the younger, English-speaking members preferred Soesterberg, while the older ones, many with a theological background, favoured Eichstätt. The question was settled by a vote, and it was apparent the result would be very close: as chair, my vote was the decisive one. I chose Soesterberg, in deep agony. This led to my secretary promptly leaving the meeting, and a break with the Catholic fundamental theologians was a fact. Since then, the theological approach has been practically absent from the conference programmes.

The Soesterberg conference was organised in 2001; there I announced that I would step down as chair and Jacob A. Belzen was elected as my successor. The following conference was held in 2003 in Glasgow and there the two groups finally merged, the opposing English-speaking group simply ceasing to exist, as they moved to take over the old organisation. This course of events is described in Belzen's grand work *Religionspsychologie*. Unfortunately, his own – sometimes dramatic – role is not all that apparent. Nevertheless, I had succeeded in achieving the goal of my occasionally very unrewarding engagement with the organisational side of the psychology of religion. There was now one single association with a long – albeit not always that glorious – history of almost 100 years, which as such is worthy of respect.

Developments have continued to happen and the conferences on the psychology of religion usually attract several hundred participants. The interest shown by scholars from the USA in the work done in Europe has grown considerably. I currently notice that experimental methodology with extensive statistical analyses seems to have become the dominant trend within research into the psychology of religion. This makes an old man like myself, with an education in both theology and psychology, wonder whether the appreciation of what religion and religiosity is will be lost when everything is reduced to entities which are only manageable by that method. To a certain extent, I observed the negative consequences of this when I carried out my study on mysticism and intense experiences (Holm, 1979).

However, the issue of the relation between religion and scientific psychological study has actually never left the research field, as the central question is: What do we, in fact, do with religion and religiosity when we explore it from a scientific perspective? Do we change religion in the course of our studies and do we enter into personal and sensitive areas when exploring religious experiences using external scientific approaches? And can we ever grasp the basic dimensions of religious experiences through our studies?

In my view, these are fundamental questions that we will never be able to totally ignore. Therefore particularly the psychology of religion is a constant struggle between on the one hand religion and religiosity as something *sui generis*, that is, basic as such, and on the other, as an object for study using modern scientific and psychological methods. We might ask ourselves whether scientific study has a detrimental impact on the occurrence and genuineness of religiosity, or whether the two approaches can exist side by side and illuminate each other reciprocally.

I will here illustrate these questions with reference to my own studies within the psychology of religion, and mainly my studies of glossolalia within the Pentecostal movement, which was the subject of my doctoral thesis at Uppsala University in 1976 (Holm, 1976).

It is a well-known fact that throughout the history of the Church, there have been movements practising what is called speaking in tongues, or glossolalia. This all goes back to the Pentecostal miracle, as described in the second chapter of the Acts of the Apostles. Tongues of fire rested on the disciples as they were gathered to pray and they began to speak in other tongues which they had never learnt. Peter stepped forward and explained that this was the descent of the Holy Spirit, something that Jesus had prophesied. According to the scriptures, a large group of people converted to the faith of Jesus that same day. The Church had been established. Through the centuries there have appeared ecstatic movements with many speakers in tongues. Often these have been exposed to persecution. However, in the beginning of the last century the Pentecostal movement experienced a strong revival and the practice of glossolalia spread extremely quickly across the entire world. Recent calculations claim that perhaps as many as approximately half a billion people have been influenced by the Pentecostal movement, or the charismatic revival.

When I wanted to study the Pentecostal movement and particularly experiences connected with glossolalia in the 1960s, there had not been very much research into the issue. Therefore I conducted field studies among Pentecostalists in the Swedish-speaking areas of Finland. I had the opportunity to make tape recordings of services during which speaking in tongues occurred and to interview individuals about their experiences of glossolalia.

My first objective was to analyse what kind of speech glossolalia was. For this purpose I had to transliterate the glossolalia and study it in comparison with ordinary speech. Identifying the individual sounds and counting the occurrence of vowels and consonants proved to be an extensive task. The results of my research can be summarised by saying that the glossolalia I encountered resembled the native language of the person who was speaking in tongues. Certain simplifications of the sound structure occurred and some exotic sounds were included. On the whole, the glossolalia was melodious, contained assonance and alliteration and sounded like poems with end rhymes. The glossolalia did not have any actual meaning in the ordinary sense, although some expressions like *satana, amen,* and *kristu* occurred. Other word-like combinations often emanated from Romance languages, particularly Latin. Examples of such forms included *stipendi, sento, santo, ponti, temporato,* and *vero*. I could not discern any real language among my recorded material, although it sometimes sounded like English or German (Holm, 1978).

What conclusions was I able to draw from the sound analysis? That the sounds of glossolalia are usually totally ordinary, in the sense that they also occur as the most basic sound structures in the native language of the speaker. This I interpreted as proof of the fact that a person who speaks a certain language also possesses abilities that can be used for producing a kind of speaking in tongues. Other examples of nonsense speech occur in jazz music and children's games. In other words, there is a high probability that humans can produce some form of mumbo jumbo speech on the basis of normal language skills if a sufficient level of motivation is present. Superficial loans from other languages are explained by natural imitation effects. I had completed a kind of psycho-linguistic study, which demonstrated a clear connection between the glossolalia and the speaker's native language with certain added exotic features.

However, for those practising glossolalia, the speaking in tongues is associated with spiritual experiences. According to the theological interpretation, one is baptised in the Holy Spirit when one starts speaking in tongues. Glossolalia is regarded as a gift of grace from God, a charisma. This is described in, for example, Paul's first epistle to the Corinthians. Speaking in tongues is therefore a deeply spiritual experience for many, with an impact lasting for years. Also, once started, the practise of glossolalia usually continues. Glossolalia is perceived as speech given by God and a channel of communication with God. In order to be able to interpret and understand the experience of speaking in tongues, that is, baptism in the Holy Spirit, I used the so-called role theory developed by Hjalmar Sundén (Holm & Belzen, 1995; Sundén, 1966). Descriptions of roles can be found in the New Testament and general behavioural models often exist in the community of the congregation.

The crucial question to be asked, then, is: Are the individual experiences of baptism in the Holy Spirit turned into something else, when it is scientifically proven that the glossolalia is a "distortion" of the speaker's native language, with certain elements of exotic sounds? As a scholar, my objective is not to change or trivialise the spiritual experience in any way. I cannot neglect my task, which is to formulate the results of my research. Some Pentecostalists who have learnt about the scientific studies, have taken them as a source of doubt and despair. Some of them have even said that if they are to be baptised in the Holy Spirit, it must happen "genuinely", that is, purely as a gift of God.

When studying a phenomenon such as glossolalia and baptism in the Holy Spirit, one therefore soon realises that the divine and the worldly are closely intertwined. Scientific research may have an impact on the qualities of the spiritual experience, although the researcher would not want that to be the case. Another insight is that there are various perspectives on reality and that these sometimes must be allowed to exist in parallel with each other. A social-constructivist approach with an appreciation of symbols will provide an opportunity for a deeper understanding of this situation (Holm, 1995; Holm, 2014). Studying religion from a psychological viewpoint will undoubtedly often put the scholar at points of intersection which may be very difficult to handle. The psychology of religion is therefore *semper militans*.

References

Belzen, J. A. (2015). *Religionspsychologie. Eine historische Analyse im Spiegel der Internationalen Gesellschaft*. Springer. Berlin Heidelberg.

Holm, N. G. (1976). *Tungotal och andedop*. Diss. Acta Universitatis Upsaliensis, Psychologia religionum 5. Uppsala.

Holm, N. G. (1978). *Pingströrelsen*. Publications of the Research Institute of the Åbo Akademi Foundation, nr 31, Åbo.

Holm, N. G. (1979). *Mystik och intensiva upplevelser*. Publications of the Research Institute of the Åbo Akademi Foundation, nr 51, Åbo.

Holm, N. G. (1995). Role theory and religious experience. In R. W. Hood, Jr., (Ed.), *Handbook of Religious Experience*. Birmingham AL: Religious Education Press.

Holm, N. G. (2014). The human symbolic construction of reality. A psycho-phenomenological study. In H. Bringeland & I. S. Gilhus (Eds.), *Nordic studies in religion and culture* (Vol. 2). LIT: Berlin.

Holm, N. G., & Belzen, J. A. (1995). *Sundén's Role Theory – An impetus to contemporary psychology of religion*. Religionsvetenskapliga skrifter nr 27. Åbo Akademi, Åbo.

Luoma, M. (1965). *Uskonnonpsykologia eilen ja tänään*. Acta academiae socialis A 1. Tampere.

Sundén, H. (1966). *Die Religion and die Rollen. Eine Psychologische Untersuchung der Frömmigkeit*. Berlin: Töpelmann.

Wulff, D. M. (1991). *Psychology of religion. Classic and contemporary views*. New York etc.: John Wiley & Sons.

CHAPTER 5

Why Wilhelm Wundt's *Völkerpsychologie* Can Hardly be Seen as an Ancestor of (Modern) Psychology of Religion

Lars Allolio-Näcke

Summary

This short commentary presents a response to Jacob Belzen's claim, Wilhelm Wundt's *Völkerpsychologie* (Vols. IV–VI) can be seen as an ancestor of (modern) psychology of religion. The paper states that *Völkerpsychologie* is not a psychological work, but rather an outdated genre of writing history of religion which was very common in the 19th century, using artifacts from all over the world that have been collected by anthropologists. In that sense Wundt cannot be claimed to have written a *psychology* of religion.

In his new book *Religionspsychologie. Eine historische Analyse im Spiegel der Internationalen Gesellschaft*, Jacob Belzen (2015) refers to Wilhelm Wundt's *Völkerpsychologie* (Vols. IV–VI) as an ancestor of the (modern) psychology of religion. This is in the same way problematic like Michael Cole (1996), who refers to the *Völkerpsychologie* as an ancestor of cultural psychology. Both strategies are clear: To establish a science or a scientific discipline there has to be not just a professorship, examination regulations and a journal (see Schönpflug & Schönpflug, 1989, p. 15), there also is the need for either a famous founder or a foundation myth – in the case of cultural psychology as well the psychology of religion that is the reference to Wilhelm Wundt's (1921b) "second psychology", which is better known as *Völkerpsychologie*.

Both "tales" are fascinating, and certainly they do have their charm – not only from the aspect of the history of science, and certainly it is smart in the sense of scientific politics. But summing up – these are tales that from a socio-historic standpoint are problematic. Wundt's beliefs of consciousness and culture are precarious, because he believed in a cultural shared soul that is more than the sum of the contemporary individual souls and transports the content of individual souls from ancient centuries too. He suggests analyzing the whole culture since the very beginning to understand the contemporary acting or thinking of the individual in religious contexts (see Stubbe, 2006,

 | DOI 10.1163/9789004322011_006

p. 43). Furthermore, his idea of culture is itself problematic, because he believed in an teleological cultural as well as religious evolutionism that starts with the "primitive" on the first level and ends with "humanitarism" on the last one (see Stubbe, 2006, p. 47).

Also problematic is his method of analyzing cultures, because it was limited to second and third analysis of cultural artifacts that had been brought along by ethno-psychologists or anthropologists; he was the Malinowski of psychology: an "armchair anthropologist" (see Zitterbarth, 2006, p. 108f.). Since the actual research that is done under the label of psychology of religion deals with lived (and not only manifested) culture and analyzes systems of signs, knowledge, rules, and symbols, Wundt in that sense could not be claimed as the father of the discipline. What can be claimed is that Wundt already saw in the very beginning of psychology that the experimental method is inappropriate to explore the higher psychic functions like fantasy, myth, religion, and custom (see Wundt, 1921a, p. 537). For that reason he thought that experimental psychology is not able to grasp the emergent and cultural matters. That was why he wrote an interpretative *Völkerpsychologie* (1921b) besides his explanatory *Experimentelle Psychologie* (1887).

As Chakkarath shows, this ambitious project remains fruitless and unread, because Wundt failed to provide his ideas with systematic and comprehensible methods (see Chakkarath, 2003, p. 37). He surely named his method genetic, but this genetic method was no method in our contemporary sense. It was more association than comparison, it was more fiction than understanding and it was at least literature not scientific report.

Furthermore, he was and remained a child of the 19th century. In the 19th century it was quite common to describe the history of religion in a teleological way. Wilhelm Wundt (1911) does not deny this way of analysis, but he saw the need to complement that analysis by a "genetic" psychology of religions:

> The duty of history is to describe the influence of various religions on the intellectual (*geistige*) development of the people. But to prove how the phenomena fit to religious ideas of the same area or of quite different and independent areas; and to prove how the religious motives at all are related to the general mental nature (*seelischen Anlagen*) of man, which is in the least not object of history of religion but psychology of religion. That is why there can be no psychology of religion without history of religion. (p. 116, translation LAN)

While the history of religion aims to describe the development as a displacement of older ideas by new ones, Wundt was looking for a "genetic" model of transformation: The new concepts do not only displace the old ideas, they took them over while transforming them on a higher new level. The movement behind is the development from the concrete/primary to the abstract/secondary:

> Claiming the religions of primitive peoples are to be excluded as a kind of "prehistory", lacks of any authorization, especially by considering the rich insights of modern ethnology on the origin and the primitive stages of the most important, in higher and spiritualized yet vivid forms of religious beliefs and cults in Christianity. (Wundt, 1911, p. 114, translation LAN)

Wundt (1911) thought that there are two methodological ways for such a genetic psychology of religion:

> A genetic psychology can either assign a number of successive stages of religious development and their transitions in ascending order that means to place individual cross sections throughout the organic context of religious history. Or it can ... draw longitudinal sections by pursuing one group of more important phenomena from the still attainable very beginnings in their transformations till now. So indispensable the first of these methods is, it must nevertheless partly prepared, partly supplemented by the second. (p. 114, translation LAN)

Even though Wundt considers the synchrony of different religious phenomena, he remains in the teleological paradigm of the 19th century. His presentation of the different phenomena aims not only on the systematization of the motives as he wrote before, but also on the creation of a hierarchy "of successive stages of religious development and their transitions in ascending order". In doing so, he denies their simultaneity by projecting them into the past. That means coexisting phenomena are interpreted as depending and successively. For this interpretation Wundt requires the described second way: the tracing of a single phenomenon in its still attainable very beginnings. For this he identifies "central spiritual motifs", ideas, and feelings, which are grouped around individual phenomena and can be found *transformed* at all stages of development; starting of course with the primitive man because of his "lowest degree of culture, especially the spiritual culture" (Wundt, 1912, p. 7, translation LAN).

Aggregated, Wundt postulates four developmental stages with its own religious practice and thinking:

Era	Religious Phenomena
Primitive Human	Archetype of belief in magic and demons Animal ancestors Bodily soul (soul is not separable from the body)
Totemistic Era	Totems of animals and plants, totems without life Genesis of taboo (the holy and the impure) Psyche as breath soul or shadow soul (soul is separable from the body) Fetish as origin of images of God; amulets and talisman Transition from animal to human ancestors Cults of death, ancestors, vegetation, acre; first signs of cults with Gods
Era of heroes and Gods	Believed myths (Epos) are transformed into Gods: God as product of the combination of heroes and demons Heroic sagas are transformed into legends of the saints Genesis of beliefs into transcendental places like Orcus, Elysian, and the heaven Genesis of the till today ongoing cultic actions: prayer, offerings, sanctification, baptism, and circumcision Ideas of the soul are transformed into beliefs into spirits or ghosts that lead to angel figures
Development of humanity (humanitarism)	Emperors as Gods; apotheosis of the Emperors Transformation of afterworld cults into cults of redemption With the idea of impersonal God the national and natural religions are transformed to world religions with the aim of Gods incarnation

In my opinion, this historical interpretations of different phenomena in one teleological row is not appropriate to grasp the reality of the historic phenomena; it is rather a projection of our ideas into the historical past. Only in this perspective they can be identified as ancestors of our contemporary phenomena; this also means to steal them their own characteristics. Additionally the coarse classification of the eras can be criticized, because they include not only one developmental step, but also a lot of them; furthermore, it can be asked if psychology started with the primitive human described this way.

Till today nobody was able to explain sufficiently where to find the roots of religion. In his book *Les Religions de la Préhistoire*, Leroi-Gourhan (1964) has convincingly deconstructed the interpretation of archeological findings for this time. There are no convincingly facts before the sedentism in the Neolithic (ca. 10,000 B.C.) that prove a religious dimension – but again and again scientist claim on artifacts (e.g., Venus of Willendorf) or cave paintings of the Upper Paleolithic to be cultic and in that sense ancestors of religion. Also traceable sepultures are not sufficient to postulate a religious dimension; the conclusion that burial objects are a sign for beliefs into an existing after the death are projections from later to this earlier times, e.g., after the mummy findings of the Egyptian pyramids.

At least, it is to consider that the idea of *Völkerpsychologie* (development of cultural thoughts and artifacts) fits just conditionally to the phenomenon of religion. It fits only for tribal cultures or religions of city-states or similar. At the latest with the development of "world religions" – that is lately with the Sumerians (on the basis of Babylonians and Assyrians) – the principles and the analytic entity are not anymore the same: the religions transcend the local and national boarders and become – with violence or peaceful – shared properties of many cultures, which also means that religion is loaded by different thoughts and idea from different systems. With this merging an internal logic of development (of religion) cannot be postulated anymore; the development has to be described furthermore out of the socio-historic conditions. For example, the differentiation of Christendom is more manifold than described by Wundt (he just knows Catholicism, Lutheranism, and Calvinism); and this differentiation is not a higher development like Wundt claims – it is just a differentiation. That means, e.g., that the decisions of the synod of Chalcedon (451) are not more developed than the rules of the Armenian apostolic church that denied the decisions of that synod. There are just different beliefs.

These are my arguments to deny that Wundt's *Völkerpsychologie* can be seen as an ancestor of (modern) psychology of religion. The real reason why his late work was not noticed is not accidental but in psychology itself no one was interested in the writing of a history of mentalities or the history of religion – this was an outdated genre of the 19th century that can be found in all new established disciplines around the centuries passage. Thus, Wundt was not a famous psychologist of religion as Jacob Belzen claims (2015, p. 45), furthermore he was a historian of religion as can be seen by a look into Wundt's reference list. All famous historians of religions are cited, but just a very few psychologists.

Beside the hard critique it is positively to underline: Wundt (1912) does not tried to focus on religion as a single phenomenon (that is the scientific dead end of our times), but tried to grasp "the main stages of psychological (*völkerpsychologisch*) development successively and each in the overall context of its phenomena" (p. 7, translation LAN). That means to outline *Principles of Psychological Development of Humankind*[1] in regard to forms of family or society, language, thinking, religion, art as well as custom (*Sitte*).

References

Belzen, J. A. (2015). *Religionspsychologie. Eine historische Analyse im Spiegel der Internationalen Gesellschaft*. Berlin, Heidelberg: Springer.

Chakkarath, P. (2003). *Kultur und Psychologie. Zur Entwicklung und Standortbestimmung der Kulturpsychologie*. Hamburg: Verlag Dr. Kovač.

Cole, M. (1996). *Cultural psychology: A once and future discipline*. Cambridge, MA: Harward University Press.

Leroi-Gourhan, A. (1964). *Les religions de la préhistoire. L'age paléolithique*. Paris: Presses Universitaires de France.

Schönpflug, W., & Schönpflug, U. (1989). *Psychologie. Allgemeine Psychologie und ihre Verzweigungen in die Entwicklungs-, Persönlichkeits- und Sozialpsychologie. Ein Lehrbuch für das Grundstudium*. München: Psychologie Verlags Union.

Stubbe, H. (2006). Die Geschichte der Völkerpsychologie. In Gerd Jüttemann (Ed.), *Wilhelm Wundts anders Erbe. Ein Missverständnis löst sich auf* (pp. 33–51). Göttingen: Vandenhoeck & Ruprecht.

Wundt, W. (1887). *Grundzüge der physiologischen Psychologie*. Leipzig: Engelmann.

Wundt, W. (1911). *Probleme der Völkerpsychologie*. Leipzig: Ernst Wiegandt.

Wundt, W. (1912). *Elemente der Völkerpsychologie. Grundlinien einer psychologischen Entwicklungsgeschichte der Menschheit*. Leipzig: Alfred Kröner.

Wundt, W. (1921a). *Kleine Schriften. Band 3*. Leipzig: Engelmann.

Wundt, W. (1921b). *Völkerpsychologie. 10 Bände*. Leipzig: Engelmann.

Zitterbarth, W. (2006). War Wundt ein Konstruktivist? In G. Jüttemann (Ed.), *Wilhelm Wundts anders Erbe. Ein Missverständnis löst sich auf* (pp. 102–115). Göttingen: Vandenhoeck & Ruprecht.

1 That is the subtitle of *Elemente der Völkerpsychologie* (1912): *Grundlinien einer psychologischen Entwicklungsgeschichte der Menschheit*.

CHAPTER 6

Some Propositions Concerning Wilhelm Stählin's Contributions to the Psychology of Religion

Erich Nestler

Summary

This paper focuses on Wilhelm Stählin in the literary style of propositions. For more elaboration and details other publications by the author may be consulted. For the newest reference for details and as a basic text see Jacob A. Belzen's book on the Psychology of Religion (Belzen, 2015).[1] As Belzen's monograph primarily takes a perspective on institutional and organizational aspects of the historical development of the psychology of religion in German speaking countries, the aim of this author is the theoretical, the methodological and the research contribution of Stählin in the field of the psychology of religion, which he considers to be a subdiscipline of psychology.

Introduction

The founder of the Archive for the Psychology of Religion and the Society for the Psychology of Religion, as it first was named, Wilhelm Stählin (1883–1975), was unique in the way he worked as a theologian within the discipline of psychology, more specifically in the areas of cognitive psychology (*Denkpsychologie*) and in the psychology of religion. The propositions presented here focus on Stählin as a psychological researcher, not as an organizer.

Propositions

P1a: Stählin belongs to the Würzburg School of Cognitive Psychology (*Denkpsychologie*, Oswald Külpe).

1 All of this author's references are based on the texts in the bibliography. Only when there is need to define a specific text, author (and year) of publication are specified in the propositions (like Wulff, 1997, or Reuschlein, 2013).

 | DOI 10.1163/9789004322011_007

P1b: He is not part of the Dorpat School (compare Wulff, 1997) of the psychology of religion. His scholarly work in the psychology of religion began historically earlier than Karl Girgensohn's, who is the central figure of the so-called Dorpat School. Stählin's theoretical foundation was in contrast to Girgensohn not theology, but psychology. He was also geographically situated in a different region. Most important though: Stählin did not build his psychological principles on theology.

P2: Stählin was the only academic protestant theologian at the time when he founded the Society for Psychology of Religion, who had earned a doctorate in psychology. Within the psychology of religion he worked with the mindset of an academically trained psychologist.

P3a: The psychology of religion is, according to Stählin, a subdiscipline of psychology. Neither the history of religions (or comparative religions) nor theology are the academic foundation of the psychology of religion.

P3b: The question of truth of religions therefore is outside the realm of the psychology of religion.

P4a: Religion is only insofar part of the work of the new academic discipline as it has to do with psychological phenomena (Stählin & Koffka, 1914, p. 1).

P4b: Concepts and theories are to be borrowed and derived from psychology. This does not preclude that results of research in the psychology of religion might be fruitful for psychology.

P5a: The research methods are the same as in psychology.

P5b: The experiment is one of the most important methods – if not the most important one – for research in the psychology of religion.

P5c: Stählin's concept of experiments is complex. His experiments could be classified as so-called qualitative experiments today (compare the work people like Ernst Mach, Gerhard Kleining, and Burkhard Vollmers). But this view comes into tension with the attempt of finding psychological laws and the use of statistics (albeit Stählin's use of statistics might be put down today as mere descriptive statistics). Therefore it does not help to call Stählin's experiments explorative or heuristic experiments on the grounds of a qualitative methodological perspective that is attempting to create new hypotheses in opposition to proving already existing hypotheses.

P5d: It might be methodologically fruitful to revisit Stählin's research in relation to his praxis of experimenting. This would entail the theoretical notions involved in his actually "doing science".

P6a: During his active time as a researcher Stählin's main interest was in the field of religious and New Testament imagery (*Bildersprache*).

P6b: His contribution to the research of metaphors, especially in relation to the theoretical concept of metaphor, is still relevant (he took an interactionist view opposed to the view of mere embellishment; Reuschlein, 2013, pp. 224–238).

P7a: Stählin's initial desire for more and deeper understanding of the religious life and experience did not get fulfilled by his scholarly research in the psychology of religion.

P7b: During World War I, Stählin came in touch with phenomenology. Including this theoretical approach in his own theoretical framework of psychology (of religion) might have helped him to overcome this conceptually rooted deficiency. This new theoretical perspective came – as far as his academic work was concerned – biographically too late.

P7c: Stählin's path into the pastoral ministry was consistent with a fundamental attitude, which already characterized his empirical research approach. Possibly one might be able to interpret his preference of the experiment as a possible indication. In the experimental approach the researcher takes on an active role of systematically influencing the "object" of interest. There is a fundamental intention to cause change. This is – on a very fundamental level – what a minister of the Gospel intends to do: to bring about change in the persons he is interacting with (and one might add, as well as him- or herself).

Conclusion

It was Belzen's (2015) strong and repeatedly stated emphasis, which made the present author fully aware of the importance of Stählin's formal academic training in psychology. Up to Belzen's publication the present author's perspective had been that Stählin was a theologian, who more or less by chance developed a taste for the new emerging academic discipline, the psychology of religion. And in developing this perspective, this present author's view took Stählin's attempt to get formal academic training in psychology as something beneficial, but not absolutely necessary. But there are so-called shibboleths, when using psychological terms and concepts, which reveal the theologian to the psychologist.[2] And vice versa concerning theological terms and concepts that a psychologist uses, who is without formal academic training in theology, stumbles upon without awareness and without even noticing the theological shibboleths. Further scrutiny by academic psychologists might test the assumption that Stählin had developed a truly psychological habitus by fully socializing into the approaches of academic psychology.

References

Belzen, J. A. (2015). *Religionspsychologie. Eine historische Analyse im Spiegel der Internationalen Gesellschaft*. Berlin/Heidelberg: Springer.

Kleining, G. (1986). Das qualitative Experiment. *Kölner Zeitschrift für Soziologie und Sozialpsychologie, 38*, 724–750.

Mach, E. (1917). *Erkenntnis und Irrtum. Skizzen zur Psychologie der Forschung* (3rd ed.; 1st ed. 1905). Leipzig: Johann Ambrosius Barth.

Nestler, E. (1986). *Der Beitrag Wilhelm Stählins zur Jugendbewegung* (Unpublished doctoral dissertation). Bayreuth.

Nestler, E. (1998). Wilhelm Stählin: Doxographie und Werkbeschreibung. In C. Henning & E. Nestler (Eds.), *Religion und Religiosität zwischen Theologie und Psychologie. Bad Boller Beiträge zur Religionspsychologie* (pp. 263–279.) Frankfurt am Main/New York: Lang.

Nestler, E. (2013). Stählin, Ernst Wilhelm. In *Neue Deutsche Biographie* (Vol. 25, pp. 24–26). Berlin: Duncker & Humblot.

2 A "shibboleth" is a mark or a sign that reveals a person's language group that she or he belongs to. It goes back to the biblical story in the Book of Judges (12:5,6). The Ephramites blocked fords at the Jordan in order that no Gileadites, with whom they were at war, could cross the river. When a Gileadite showed up they asked to which tribe he belonged. When he would claim that he did not belong to the Gileadites, they would tell him to say the word for corn or grain (in Hebrew). Would the person pronounce it "sibboleth" (instead of "shibboleth"), they would know to which tribe the passenger belonged. So in metaphorical usage the term means "sign" or "mark".

Reuschlein, N. (2013). *Biblische Metaphern und Grundschulkinder. Eine qualitative empirische Studie zum Verständnis ausgewählter Ich-bin-Worte in Kinderbildern.* Bamberg: University of Bamberg Press.

Stählin, W. (1913). Zur Psychologie und Statistik der Metaphern. Eine methodologische Untersuchung. Leipzig/Berlin: Engelmann. (Würzburg Phil. Diss. 1913; reprint from *Archiv für die gesamte Psychologie, 31*(1), p. 129).

Stählin, W. (1914). Experimentelle Untersuchungen über Sprachpsychologie und Religionspsychologie. *Archiv für Religionspsychologie, 1*, 117–194.

Stählin, W., & Koffka, K. (1914). Zur Einführung. *Archiv für Religionspsychologie, 1*, 1–9.

Vollmers, B. (1992). *Kreatives Experimentieren. Die Methodik von Jean Piaget, den Gestaltpsychologen und der Würzburger Schule.* Wiesbaden: Deutscher Universitäts-Verlag.

Wulff, D. (1997). *Psychology of religion. Classic & contemporary* (2nd ed.). New York: Wiley.

CHAPTER 7

Searching for the Holy Grail: The Elusive Identity of Psychology of Religion

Troels Nørager

Summary

Jacob Belzen's *Religionspsychologie* is the first in-depth study of the history of the IAPR. Being a first-rate scholarly work within the history of psychology of religion, it has uncovered a lot of hitherto unknown material, as well as providing us with fascinating portraits of the little known (mostly German) founding figures of the organization and its journal, the *Archiv für Religionspsychologie*. Belzen, however, turns out to be more than just a historian. He also intends to use the historical outline as a mirror for reflecting on the elusive identity of psychology of religion past and present. This invited commentary falls into three parts. First, and drawing upon *The Varieties* of William James, an interpretive context for the emergence of psychology of religion is presented. Second, the question is raised as to what kind of lesson we may learn from the admirable historical analysis presented in *Religionspsychologie*. Third, I end my commentary by questioning whether psychology of religion really needs a (more or less) fixed identity. Perhaps, to continue looking for *the* identity of such a diverse field may prove as futile as the search for the Holy Grail?

Introduction

Jacob Belzen has taken the centenary of the International Association for Psychology of Religion (IAPR) as a proper occasion for presenting us with an in-depth study of its history. As it turns out, this is a somewhat troubled (and troubling) story raising serious questions to anyone interested in psychology of religion. And raising questions and encouraging debate is very much what Belzen's book is all about. Having correctly noted that there are surprisingly few studies of the history of psychology of religion, Belzen states his primary intention as follows: "Wie angegeben, will unsere Studie letztlich zur Reflexion auf die Religionspsychologie beitragen. Was ist sie überhaupt: eine Wissenschaft, eine Disziplin, ein Fachgebiet, eine Zunft oder was für ein Unternehmen?" (Belzen, 2015, p. 7). Indeed, what *is* psychology of religion, when all is said and

 | DOI 10.1163/9789004322011_008

done? We shall return to this question below, but let me first offer a more general characterization of the book.

As the subtitle indicates, Belzen has wisely chosen to use the development of the *Gesellschaft* (and its organ *Archiv für Religionspsychologie*) from 1914 onwards as a mirror reflecting (and for reflecting upon) the history of psychology more generally. This may sound surprising, for although clearly aiming to become *the* international association that it is today, the *Gesellschaft* in its founding period was very much a German enterprise. Still, Belzen accomplishes nothing less than providing us with the hitherto most comprehensive account of European psychology of religion. This is in itself a major achievement, since previous histories of psychology of religion have tended to overlook the European scene (with Wulff, 1997, as a major exception). Besides, in the process he has uncovered a lot of hitherto unknown material and acquainted us with persons who used to be no more than just names. It cannot be emphasized enough that Belzen's well-written account elegantly hides the fact that it is based upon many years of serious (and probably often tedious) work demanding the study of sources in several libraries and archives (a long list is provided in the book). This truly amazing achievement combined with an impressive attention to detail makes this book a truly scholarly work. I think it only fair to add that this almost super-human task could only be accomplished by someone with the rare expertise and extensive knowledge like Belzen, who has devoted his entire career to furthering the cause of psychology of religion. Throughout the book, he displays a stunning knowledge of all varieties of the field and its booming literature right up to the present day. Clearly, this is a book written by someone who is *au courant* with what is going on in the many different corners of psychology of religion.

The following brief commentary and reflection on Belzen's book falls into three parts. In the first section, I present an interpretive context for the emergence of psychology of religion as a scientific enterprise. Second, I want to address the question of what kind of lessons we may learn from the historical analysis so admirably carried out by Belzen. Briefly put: Is there a moral to this story? Third, and finally, I end up discussing to what extent psychology of religion *needs* an identity. Before we proceed, however, a certain *caveat* seems appropriate: This commentary is written by someone whose professional identity is not that of a psychologist of religion. Instead, I am a systematic theologian from Denmark with a long-standing interest in the field. My defense here would be double: First, that sometimes outsiders see more clearly, and second that Belzen himself has demonstrated (as I imagine to the surprise of many) how the early psychology of religion (and the IAPR) was to a large extent embedded in an attempt to readjust theology to the demands of a modern world. Whether this theological interference has been a boon or bane to psychology of religion is of course a matter for debate.

Theologians on a Mission: Searching for the Holy Grail

Regarding the early, founding phase around 1914, Belzen's account is at the same time a fascinating insight into parts of theology, since theologians were among the first to embrace the impulses coming from the USA. While the empirical results of the Clark school were duly noted, it was first and foremost William James' *The Varieties of Religious Experience* (1902) that stimulated the interest of many liberal-minded theologians looking for new ways of approaching religion. Instead of dogma and church, the interest turned to individual experience. This is clearly reflected in Harald Høffding's (himself an acquaintance of James) preface to the first Danish edition from 1906; in characterizing James' focus Høffding writes, "It is the inner, personal side of religion that occupies him – the side that can make it independent of all dogmas and institutions, and without which these are but empty shells".[1] But what *is* this "inner, personal side of religion"? The answer is as straightforward as it is significant: It is the individual, *human heart* so regularly referred to in religious language. Characteristic of Christian tradition since Augustine is that it is steeped in heart-language: All aspects of faith (sin, repentance, conversion, salvation, etc.) are experienced and expressed by referring to the heart. Obviously, this focus can be found in other religions as well, but its particular prominence in Christianity may stem from the tendency to conceptualize the God-man relation as one of mutual *love*. Now, what are the implications of this for understanding the emergence of psychology of religion? It means that many of the pioneers were on a mission searching for the Holy Grail, i.e., for a way to describe and express in psychological terms what religious language referred to the heart (and soul).[2]

In *Varieties*, this duality or tension between on the one hand a religious folk model of the mind and on the other hand an attempt to develop a scientific

1 Quoted from James (1963, p. 5, my translation). Villiam Grønbæk had prepared this abridged, second Danish publication of *Varieties*, and it is a telling testimony to his life-long allegiance to Werner Gruehn and the Dorpat School that in his "Introduction" to the new Danish edition of 1963, he refers to Gruehn's *Die Frömmigkeit der Gegenwart* (1956) as "the contemporary standard work in psychology of religion" (quoted from James, 1963, p. 7, my translation).

2 The relation between heart language and psychological language as different models of the mind is the subject of my habilitation *Hjerte og Psyke* [Heart and Psyche] (Nørager, 1996).

model is clearly displayed. James quotes extensively from his human documents (heart language) and attempts to subject them to a psychological interpretation and explanation. And what is of particular interest here is the fact that James himself was aware of this duality or tension. Thus, in a letter describing his own impression of the Gifford Lectures at Ediburgh (subsequently to be published as *Varieties*) he writes to a friend:

> The audience was extraordinarily attentive and reactive – I never had an audience so keen to catch every point. I flatter myself that by blowing alternately hot and cold on their Christian prejudices I succeeded in baffling them completely till the final quarter-hour, when I satisfied their curiosity by showing more plainly my hand. Then, I think, I permanently dissatisfied both extremes, and pleased a mean numerically quite small.[3]

What we may learn from this is that the fascination of *Varieties* stems from its complex strategy of combining "hot" parts of religious heart-language with "cold" parts of psychological explanation (cf. Nørager, 1995). But in a broader perspective, much more is at stake. For just as psychology general has a prehistory of folk (and philosophical) models of the mind, psychology of religion is faced with the task of somehow competing with the religious self-descriptions. If this task is not solved successfully, we may end up (just like James himself feared) only pleasing "a mean numerically quite small".

The task in question, obviously, is a *hermeneutical* one of translation and interpretation, of moving freely between religious self-descriptions and scientific distance. This is what James accomplished so successfully in *Varieties* and what in my opinion goes a long way in accounting for its continuing status as a classic. It is a matter of handling different language games and perspectives. This, however, was not how psychology of religion was perceived by those with formative influence on the early history of the IAPR. The hypothesis I wish to put forward here is that contrary to the philosophical pragmatist James (who focused on the *varieties*), the German theologian-psychologists were on a quest, searching for something much more *specific*: the Holy Grail of Christian faith-experience. This is signaled already in the title of Girgensohn's *Der seelische Aufbau des religiösen Erlebens* (1925). What Girgensohn hopes to accomplish, armed with the experimental method he learned by Oswald Külpe, is nothing less than discovering the very anatomy of religious experience. Everything had to be "scientific" to boot: Stimulus-word (German: *Reizwort*) presented to students (more often than not students of theology) and the exact measuring of reaction time.

3 Letter from James to Charles Eliot Norton, quoted from Bowers (1985, p. 544).

My own compatriot Villiam Grønbæk (1897–1970) went to Berlin and learned this experimental method from Werner Gruehn, Girgensohn's loyal disciple. And Grønbæk, in turn, remained loyal to Gruehn. The experimental design was used in his habilitation (Grønbæk, 1935) where his goal was nothing less than a precise, psychological description of the very core of religious experience. Here we see the scientistic self-misunderstanding at work: Grønbæk really *believed* that he discovered the Holy Grail; what he was *actually* doing, however, was translating the heart-language of Christian tradition into psychological terms. Thus, his major result was introducing the term "centralmomenter" [central elements] to replace what Girgensohn and Gruehn called "I-functions" (German: *Ich-Funktionen*). The defining feature of centralmomenter, according to Grønbæk, is that the "central" and "deep" in personality is being touched and becoming active. In other words, what we have is an attempt to translate the religious folk model of heart-language into an allegedly scientific language. But is this latter language better or more informative than heart-language? In the case of Grønbæk and the Dorpat School, I fail to see that this is the case.

But has heart language not become obsolete? Is it not a thing of the past? No, we just don't think very much about it. Nonetheless, it is still a dominant folk model of the mind. How do I know that? It is evident from the fact that our popular music regularly refers to the heart when it (sort of like a modern continuation of the Old Testament psalms) laments about the troubles of (mostly unhappy) love. Besides, in the texts of popular music we also regularly come across references to God. From this we may learn that there is a close, internal connection between *religion* (or better: religious longing) and human *love*. Perhaps a study of God-talk in popular music would be a worthwhile empirical task for future psychology of religion?

What Can We Learn from the History of Psychology of Religion?

I have spent some time on this objectivist trend so characteristic of the Dorpat School, because I see it as having exercised a rather harmful influence on the early phases of the IAPR. If we add to this the contingent factor of particular persons (the paranoid and extremely difficult Gruehn, who only tolerated the so-called experimental psychology of religion), we may be able to explain why the *Gesellschaft* and its *Archiv* had the troubled history that Belzen has so masterfully presented to us.[4]

4 Regarding the extremely difficult personality of Gruehn, Belzen's account confirms findings based upon the correspondence between Gruehn and Grønbæk (cf. Nørager, 2000).

And yet we may also want to ask the contra-factual question of what could or might have occurred instead of all that went wrong. In this respect, chapter 5, devoted to what Belzen, with an expression from Gruehn, calls "the fiercest battle" (*schärfster Kampf*) in psychology of religion, is of particular interest. Here (Belzen, 2015, pp. 89 ff.) we are introduced to the highly gifted married couple Karl and Marianne Beth in Vienna who regularly gathered people interested in psychology of religion and in 1924 established yet another international association, including their own journal, *Zeitschrift für Religionspsychologie*, in other words, an obvious competition to the German enterprise led by Gruehn. The competition became even more serious in 1931, when the Austrian society managed to arrange an impressive, international conference in Vienna. Gruehn and Beth negotiated a merger between the two associations but the attempt failed. One cannot help wondering what might have been, had the two men been able to find common ground and join forces. Anyway, I am grateful to Belzen for having introduced me to the Beths.

But in general (and as mentioned earlier), I regard it as a major merit of Belzen's book that he gives flesh and blood to what used to be just odd names. In presenting the many persons involved in the early history of IAPR, a distinction is made between a number of theologians who are designated as forerunners (German: *im Vorfeld*), and thus not belonging to the field of psychology of religion itself: these include names like Vorbrodt, Bresler, Runze, and Wobbermin. The reason behind this is that according to Belzen, the "birth" of psychology of religion proper comes only when professional *psychologists* enter the field (Belzen, 2015, pp. 45 ff.). But is this limitation really justified?

What is the overall lesson that Belzen draws from his own impressive account? Should we mourn the history of the IAPR? At this point I want to quote part of his evaluation:

> Aus dem vorangehenden Teil kann man zumindest zweierlei lernen, einerseits, wie heterogen die Ansichten über so etwas wie Religionspsychologie sind, andererseits, dass zu deren Determinanten und Grundlagen weit mehr gehören als nur jene philosophisch-theologischen Voraussetzungen, die gewöhnlich in reflexiven Werken zur Religionspsychologie behandelt werden. (Belzen, 2015, p. 195).

But what *is* psychology of religion, strictly speaking? Belzen admonishes us that: "Längst nicht alles, was sich zwischen den beiden Polen 'Religion' und 'Psychologie' bewegt, ist Religionspsychologie; Religionspsychologie ist eigentlich nur ein ganz kleiner Teil aus diesem Bereich." (Belzen, 2015, p. 196). In other words, we seem to be left with a very small field, indeed. Let us turn, therefore, to looking a bit closer into the issue of the elusive identity of psychology of religion.

Does Psychology of Religion Need an Identity?

As already indicated, with the last chapter of Belzen's *Religionspsychologie*, historical analysis gives way to the somewhat looser and explorative form of an essay. Having presented us in the previous chapters with a plethora of rich, historical accounts and insights, the time has now come to listen to what the master himself makes of all this (*Beobachtungen und Betrachtungen*). The keyword in this respect is *pluriformity*, for the historical analysis has demonstrated the extent to which psychology of religion takes on many different forms in terms of object, purpose and approach of the researcher, as well as cultural background and context. In other words, the *identity* of psychology of religion remains elusive, at best. Should this worry us? Does psychology of religion really need a more fixed and stable identity?

Before returning to this question, let us follow Belzen in taking stock of the results of the more than hundred-year-old *Gesellschaft*. What did it accomplish? Certainly less than one might have hoped for. Belzen acknowledges that not only has the IAPR not been able to integrate all European contributions to the field but also that (even despite his own efforts) it is virtually unknown ("so gut wie nicht bekannt") among American psychologists of religion. Hence his modest conclusion: "Mit ihren gut 200 Mitgliedern ist die IAPR sicherlich keine wichtige Organisation in den Welten von Psychologie, Religionswissenschaft und verwandten Bereichen" (Belzen, 2015, p, 194 f.).

The impression I get from Belzen's book, and in particular from the concluding essay, is that pluriformity is what he sees when he looks around at what is going on and being published under the label "psychology of religion". But at the same time I detect a certain sadness or perhaps an unwillingness to accept that this may be as good as it gets. Hence, Belzen's search for a remedy in terms of attempting to clarify (and propose as binding to everyone?) a particular (but at the same time elusive) identity of psychology of religion. But is this the answer? Is this the right way to proceed? I doubt that, not least because the early history of IAPR that Belzen has so impressively traced and detailed for us, demonstrates the detrimental effects of wanting to limit psychology of religion to one particular version. Not to mention the fact that what was intended to be strictly experimental and very scientific was actually not scientific but, rather, a translation from heart-language to a quasi-scientific language.

In describing the controversy between the "forerunner" Wobbermin and the "pioneer" Stählin, Belzen clearly sides with the latter and faults theologians for (mis)using psychology of religion to promote a certain kind of religion. It cannot be denied that this, often coupled with apologetic motives, has been the case but if what they say is interesting and illuminating, should we really deny it a fair hearing? This *restrictive* trend in Belzen, trying so hard to delineate an identity amidst all the pluriformity, also comes to the fore when he comments on James' *Varieties*. Thus, on page 199 he presents it as belonging to a category of non-psychology (literature and the arts, more generally) where, as he candidly admits, the master-works often teach us more about the human predicament than psychology proper. But if this is true, and here I concur with Belzen, should that not give us occasion to ponder self-critically?[5]

Belzen returns to *Varieties* once again on page 236 commenting that, "Das Meisterwerk von James erwies sich als eher literarisch und spekulativ als psychologisch" (Belzen, 2015, p. 236). But is it really good advice to ban all that is speculative from psychology of religion? That would mean throwing psychoanalytic approaches out the window, and suddenly a psycho-biographic classic like Erikson's *Young Man Luther* (also mentioned in Belzen's book) would no longer belong to psychology of religion. Is that the kind of purification we need? And what about Belzen's own book, does that properly belong to psychology of religion? It would be somewhat ironic if that were not the case, since its title is *Religionspsychologie*. And yet it does not meet Belzen's own requirement of applying psychological theory or method to religious phenomena.

Be that as it may, Belzen clearly wants to emphasize that psychology of religion is based upon psychology: "Die Religionspsychologie ist vital abhängig von ihrer Mutterdisziplin". And then, almost as an apology, he adds: "Sie kann nicht besseres leisten, als die Psychologie ihr zu leisten ermöglicht" (Belzen, 2015, p. 237). And as everyone knows, psychology has no "identity", so how should psychology of religion be able to have one? Another critical factor is mentioned on page 211 where Belzen refers to "die zunehmenden Tabuisierung der Religion innerhalb der Psychologie". This is not just a recent trend; right from its beginnings religion was a taboo in psychology because of fear that the repressed would return in one form or other.

To me, an important lesson from Belzen's *Religionspsychologie* is that we need a different and more *open* model for thinking about what psychology of

5 In the same vein, some pages later Belzen again hints at religious literature more generally and says: "Es sei von vornherein zugegeben, dass vieles vom Genannten wesentlich interessanter, sogar aufschlussreicher als die Religionspsychologie sein mag" (Belzen, 2015, p. 217).

religion is all about. In my opinion, psychology of religion is the attempt to establish constructive, academic dialogue between the world of psychology and the world of religion. No more, no less. Consequently, we might as well stop lamenting or even mourning the elusive identity of the field. Let us agree that "pluriformity" is a *normal* and even potentially healthy situation that we also find in disciplines like anthropology, theology, and religious studies. Thus, instead of trying to limit the number and scope of different approaches, we ought to demand that each and every publication in the field should be able to answer at least the following questions: How is this particular research/study *interesting*? What is its *significance*? How does it contribute to existing knowledge? What *difference* does it make?

In addition, perhaps we should get more used to distinguishing between *theoretical* (including historical studies like Belzen's) and *empirical* psychology of religion. To me, the perhaps most important lesson from Belzen's impressive study (although probably unintended by the author himself) is that it is hard to see why we should *a priori* exclude philosophical and theological contributions (like Vorbrodt or Wobbermin) from theoretical psychology of religion. And with respect to Wobbermin, I wish to conclude this commentary with a quotation that made a particular impression on me; Belzen says of Wobbermin that:

> Manchmal stritt er geradezu ab, dass die von ihm besprochenen Werke überhaupt Religionspsychologie leisteten: Es handle sich zum Beispiel bei den Arbeiten aus der Clark-Schule (Hall, Starbuck, Leuba und andere) "um allgemeine Psychologie, nur speziell für das Gebiet des religiösen Lebens. Aber das ist noch nicht *Religions-Psychologie*, noch nicht Psychologie des religiösen Bewusstseins in seiner spezifisch religiösen Eigenart". (Wobbermin 1911/1913, S. 65, Hervorhebung im Original; Belzen, 2015, p. 43)

Hence my question to Belzen (and to all of us who take an interest in psychology of religion): Is it conceivable that Wobbermin may have a valid point?

References

Belzen, J. A. (2015). *Religionspsychologie. Eine historische Analyse im Spiegel der Internationalen Gesellschaft*. Berlin und Heidelberg: Springer Verlag.

Bowers, F. (1985). The text of *The Varieties of Religious Experience*. In F. H. Burkhardt, F. Bowers, & I. K. Skrupskelis (Eds.), *The varieties of religious experience* by William James (pp. 520–587). Cambridge, MA: Harvard University Press.

Grønbæk, V. (1935). *Om Beskrivelsen af religiøse Oplevelser* [On Describing Religious Experience]. København: Gads Forlag.

James, W. (1963). *Religiøse erfaringer* [Religious Experience] (T. H. Andersen, Trans.). København: Jespersen og Pios Forlag.

Nørager, T. (1995). Blowing alternately hot and cold: William James and the complex strategies of *The Varieties*. In D. Capps & J. L. Jacobs (Eds.), *The struggle for life: A companion to William James's the varieties of religious experience* (Society for the Scientific Study of Religion, Monograph Series, Number 9, pp. 61–71). Newton, Kansas: Mennonite Press.

Nørager, T. (1996). *Hjerte og Psyke. Studier i den religiøse oplevens metapsykologi og diskurs* [Heart and Psyche: Studies on the Metapsychology and Discourse of Religious Experience]. København: Forlaget Anis.

Nørager, T. (2000). Villiam Grønbaek and the Dorpat School: Elements of a "history" based on the correspondence between Villiam Grønbaek and Werner Gruehn. In J. A. Belzen (Ed.), *Aspects in contexts – Studies in the history of psychology of religion*, (pp. 173–233). Amsterdam & Atlanta, GA: Editions Rodopi.

Wulff, D. M. (1997). *Psychology of religion: Classic and contemporary*. New York: John Wiley & Sons.

CHAPTER 8

Traugott Konstantin Oesterreich: An Early Pioneer of the Psychology of Religion

Uwe Wolfradt and Sarah Demmrich

Summary

This contribution discusses the concept of psychology of religion by Traugott Konstantin Oesterreich (1880–1949), who analyzed religiosity in the tradition of French psychopathology and German philosophy. Inspired by William James, the main focus of his research was on individual religious experience. He considered dissociative processes (such as depersonalization and derealization) as the foundation of mystical and ecstatic experiences. Employing different religious phenomena, like glossolalia, inspiration, and states of possession, Oesterreich assumed that ego division and trance experiences are necessary to understand the development of religiosity in different cultures. Furthermore, Oesterreich emphasized parapsychology for the interpretation of religious experiences. Oesterreich's approach to examine religiosity in terms of dissociative mechanisms is discussed in relation to contemporary research.

Introduction

Although Traugott Konstantin Oesterreich was not a member of the International Association for the Psychology of Religion, founded in 1914, he actively participated in the discussions within the new discipline. How important is the transcendence in mystical and ecstatic experience? This was an essential question in the scientific context of psychology of religion at that time. At the 8th International Congress for Psychology (ICP) in Groningen, a dispute between the American psychologist James Henry Leuba and Oesterreich took place. He critisized that Leuba considered the issue in a stricktly scientific way. Instead, Oesterreich emphasized that besides pure psychological explanations for religious experiences (e.g., the theory of the unconscious), theories of religious studies and parapsychology are justified (perception of the divine; see Belzen, 2015).

Oesterreich was a member of the scientific board of the *Zeitschrift für Religionspsychologie* (Journal for the Psychology of Religion, founded in 1928) and

 | DOI 10.1163/9789004322011_009

can be characterized as a "God seeker", who did not want to distinguish sharply between psychology of religion and philosophy of religion. Stimulated by reading the book *The Varieties of Religious Experience* by William James (1902/1985), he regarded religious experience as crucial for the psychology of religion. He approached the subject following Rudolf Hermann Lotze's, a German philosopher, philosophy of value. Based on his own theory of feelings and monadological ego-theory, Oesterreich analyzed religious experience and encouraged parapsychological interpretations of religious phenomena. He considered ecstatic and mystical experience as an immediate connection to the divine and he tried to verify the different encounters with the immanent divine in diverse cultures (Christian, Hindu, Buddhist, small-scale societies). His interest in metaphysics led him to a pantheistic understanding of God, similar to the one of German romanticists.

The Biography of Traugott Konstantin Oesterreich (1880–1949)

Traugott Konstantin Oesterreich was born in September 15, 1880 in Stettin (now: Szczecin in Poland) as the son of a Prussian ministry official. He spent his childhood and adolescence in Berlin, where he finished secondary school in 1899. In the same year he began to study mathematics, physics, and astronomy at the University of Berlin. Two years later, he switched to philosophy and psychology and graduated in 1905. The title of his PhD-thesis is "Kant and the Metaphysics" (*Kant und die Metaphysik*), supervised by Friedrich Paulsen and Carl Stumpf. From 1905 to 1910, Oesterreich worked as a private scholar at the Neurobiological Institute in Berlin together with the physician Oskar Vogt. There he became familiar with the history of philosophy and the German and French psychopathology. These studies led to his habilitation "The Phenomenology of the Ego in Its Fundamental Problems" (*Die Phänomenologie des Ich in ihren Grundproblemen*), which he submitted in 1910 at University of Tübingen. Between 1910 and 1922, Oesterreich was working as an associate professor (Privatdozent) and since 1916 as an extraordinary professor in Tübingen. Oesterreich became a full professor of philosophy and psychology in Tübingen in 1922. There he founded the psychological institute between 1924 and 1930. Because he was denounciated for his early advocacy supporting democracy in Germany during the Weimar Republic, for his pacifistic attitude, and his marriage to a Jewish woman, Oesterreich was early retired with a reduced pension by the Nazi Government in 1933. Oesterreich and his wife and daughter suffered under poor material conditions and the harassments by the NS-Regime (house searching, interrogations, threat of deportation). After the Second

World War, Oesterreich was rehabilitated and became full professor again; however, this was revoked in 1947. This forced retirement led to two strokes with paralyses of which he died on July 28, 1949. Oesterreich can be described as a humble, reluctant, nearly inhibited man, who immersed himself in the scientific work as an academic maverick. He was considered as an old type scholar and theorist, who had difficulties in relating to others. As a religious man he was awestruck by the great things and questions, according to his wife Maria Oesterreich (1954).

His Philosophy of Life in the Context of Psychology

Oesterreich was interested in problems of cultural psychology and the psychology of religion. Starting from the French psychopathology (later also American psychopathology) he got into the research of dissociative aspects of human experience, ego-estrangement, and ego-split (depersonalization) (see Oesterreich, 1928; Wolfradt, 2003). His focus was on self-esteem and its clinical deviations. It was of utmost importance to him to fight against the mechanistic world view (see Oesterreich, 1925), which follows from a naturalistic concept of reality and which does not assign any discrete entity to mental states. Because of his interest in metaphysical and religious problems, he applied clinical theories to the psychology of religion (e.g., when dealing with phenomena of possession) and parapsychology (e.g., when dealing with media and occult apparitions). Additionally, he discovered early the influence of emotions on human behavior and developed his own theory of feeling (Oesterreich, 1906/07). Moreover, he was internationally one of the most famous researchers in the field of parapsychology in the 1920s. Thus, some of his works were translated into several languages (e.g., Oesterreich, 1921). In Germany, parapsychology was not highly appreciated by most scientists (with the exception of a few researchers, such as Hans Driesch), which lead to Oesterreich's isolation within German speaking academic psychology. In addition to his cultural psychological and parapsychological studies, Oesterreich conducted basic perception experiments (color perception, geometrical-visual illusions), which were acknowledged in German psychology.

Depersonalization and the Consciousness of Personality

Oesterreich (1906/07) emphasized that every human perception is accompanied by feelings (sensual and cognitive) and imaginations. He stated that during psychasthenia – a concept by Pierre Janet, in which the function of reality (*fonction de reél*) is reduced – the feelings of activity (*Aktivitätsgefühle*) are inhibited. This causes changed impressions of perception (*Wahrnehmungseindrücke*) and feelings of estrangement regarding one's personality and body (depersonalization). This disturbance of personality awareness manifests itself in a paradoxical experience of emotional emptiness with affective hyperarousal at the same time (see Wolfradt, 2003). In his model of psychasthenia already Janet had described the decrease of the mental capability of synthesis in the development of depersonalization (Wolfradt, 2006). For Oesterreich, the processes of dissociaton, depersonalization, and derealization do not only constitute the base of psychopathological disturbances, but also of nonpathological forms of experience in religious and occult phenomena. Forms of ego division (*dédoublement de personalité*) are often the precondition for mystical and ecstatic experience. Here, the individual experiences a feeling of estrangement, which manifests itself either in one obsessive emotion ("it thinks in me") or in two coexisting states of emotions. Consequently, experiences of conversion such as those of Paul the apostle in front of the gates of Damascus (his transformation "from Saul to Paul") obtain a psychological explanation. Oesterreich represented here Leibniz' monadological ego theory, i.e., the ego is not a composite of ego elements (as in the theory of association by David Hume), but has a continous substance: every mental state and act contain the ego as a whole (Oesterreich, 1910; Wolfradt, 2010). In an ecstatic or mystical state the feelings of grief and happiness can occur simultaneously without the loss of the ego's experience of continuity. However, the affects can be so strong that the feeling of ego division emerges as the presence of two mental entities.

Religiosity in the Context of Dissociative Experiences

In addition to Traugott Konstantin Oesterreich's habilitation *Die Phänomenologie des Ich* (Vol. 1, 1910) and his second volume to *The Phenomenology of the I* (1937, unpublished), he has contributed three important writings to the psychology of religion: "The religious experience as a philosophical problem" (*Die religiöse Erfahrung als philosophisches Problem*, 1915), "Introduction to the Psychology of Religion" (*Einführung in die Religionspsychologie*, 1917) and "The possession" (*Die Besessenheit*, 1921). Oesterreich characterized religiosity by its relations to life, i.e., the relations of mind and will to superhuman entities, which can be an object of personal experience, but must be definitely acknowledged as existing ("das heißt in Gemüts- und Willensbeziehungen zu übermenschlichen Wesenheiten, die unter Umständen, aber nicht notwendig auch

Gegenstand einer persönlichen Erfahrung sein können, auf jeden Fall aber als existierend anerkannt werden müssen"; 1917, p. 17). Superhuman entities are of pure spiritual nature, even if the belief is directed towards objects, which are seen as animated (e.g., amulets). Consequently, Oesterreich considered the transition from religious to occult phenomena as fluent.

Religious experiences reflect specific experiences of value (*Werterlebnisse*) and lead to metaphysical thoughts. However, these experiences of value are bounded to acts of faith (e.g., prayer): Religious experience of value requires faith. Unlike fantasy, where an inner distance to the object of faith exists, authentic religious experience is characterized by a deep emotional touch (mental devotion to the content of faith).

According to Oesterreich, the recognition of a metaphysical system can be facilitated through religious experiences. Using self-reports and narratives of mystics, he showed that an intensity of the experience of God becomes apparent, within which the work of God in the human being is considered of the highest value. God does not only enter in, but pervades the consciousness of a person. Oesterreich emphazised here the separation between immediate experience and the interpretation of the experience. Religious experience is characterized by inspiring affect (highest feeling of value). However, this experience can also be seen as a dissociative phenomenon that he considered as an affective process of obsession. The individual feels helpless, because being at the mercy of the divine, who speaking to her (glossolalia), inducing acts (inspiration), or sending messages (visions). Then, forms of ego-estrangement (depersonalization) and automatic behaviors (psychological automatism according to Janet) become manifested in religious experience. Visions can be distinguished in hallucinatory visions (internal image without any relationship to the objective reality), imaginative visions (internal imagination with a relationship to the objective reality), and intuitive visions (abstract thinking processes, e.g., feeling of the presence of God). Unlike visions, Oesterreich considered illusions as real perceptions, which are deformed by fantasies (misjudgement of reality). Visions can occur both while being awake and while dreaming. Additionally, he classified visions regarding the place (in the personal environment or distance) and the time (present, future, and past). The contents of the visions can be aestethic (positive) or apocalytic (negative). According to Oesterreich, the purpose of visions is to gain insights to the trancendent world and therefore they can broaden the perception. Finally, he described glossolalia as automated talking in a dissociative state, which cannot be remembered. The talks can be meaningful, in a foreign language, or in artificial languages.

Oesterreich postulated a phylogenetic theory of religious development – he distinguished the stage of sublimity (*Erhabenheit*) from the stage of ethical deity (*Sittlichkeit der Gottheit*). The first stage reflects the power of the divine, while God becomes an ideal image of peace and all-encompassing love at the second stage (moral enhancement of the idea of God). The fear of God changes to awe and admiration when higher developmental stages are reached. The relationship of the individual to God is internalized and accompanied by contemplation. Oesterreich referred to Buddhism and Hinduism as examples of religiosity without a monotheistic God: "The relation of the individual to this highest being is that of longing, to dissolve oneself in this being means salvation of the individual existence" ("Das Verhältnis des Individuums zu diesem höchsten Etwas ist das der Sehnsucht, die Auflösung darin bedeutet die Erlösung von der Existenz des Individuums", 1917, p. 148).

The relationship between psychology of religion and parapsychology takes an important role in the approach to this topic: Prophecies in the religious context represent forms of clairvoyance, which is similar to an intuitive empathy towards others. Through suggestion and autosuggestion a variety of religious as well as parapsychic phenomena can be explained. Humans follow voluntarily suggestions of others or encourage themselves by affirmations (e.g., in prayers, formula of faith). Nevertheless, Oesterreich considered parapsychology not as a hard science, which can support the science of religion because most of the parapsychological hypotheses had not yet been supported by empirical studies. However, the openness to parapsychology depends on the worldview of the time and of the scientists involved.

Mental states of possession form an essential part among diverse phenomena from the perspective of the psychology of religion. Approaching these states, Oesterreich examined reports from Europe and other regions of the world. During states of possession the organism feels controlled by an alien internal force, i.e., a second soul is present in the body of the person concerned. Additionally, the appearance of the possessed person changes as he gets a physiognomia, which is similiar to the alien – mostly male – person and has an altered voice (higher pitch). The content of the speaking is rough and violates ethical and religious conceptions of society.

The possessed person empathizes with gods, demons, deceased, and animals (wolves, dogs, cats, etc.: zooanthropia), being in a state of highest motor and affective excitement within which everything runs automatically, without control. Oesterreich distinguished between two forms of possession: the somnambulant (demonic) and the lucid possession. While in the somnambulant possession the consciousness and the memory of the possessed person do not exist, the normal consciousness of personality remains in the lucid form and the person concerned is aware of the possessing spirit. According to Oesterreich, dissociative phenomena play also an essential role within these states of possession because during the somnambulant possession the person experiences an involuntary and obsessive occupation of a spirit. Furthermore, states of trance in spiritualistic media are closely related to states of possession: At this point the modern world comes into contact with the religiosity of the primitive sphere (ancestors, belief in spirits; Oesterreich, 1921).

In his unpublished manuscript "The Phenomenology of the I" (*Die Phänomenologie des Ich*, Vol. II), which was written in 1937, Oesterreich discussed ecstatic experiences. He raised the question whether ecstatic experiences represent more than pure experiences of value, namely a real internal relationship to God. According to Oesterreich ecstasy cannot be explained merely in physiological terms (for instance as a consequence of physical exhaustion or physical well-being), but can be understood when including parapsychological knowledge (e.g., mediumism). Additionally, he developed a phenomenology of ecstacy in developmental stages (from the stage of humbleness to the stage of the supernatural). It is evident that Oesterreich was not interested in pathologization of religious experiences, but rather in nonpathological dissociative experiences that are the basis for religious and occult phenomena.

To the Significance of T. K. Oesterreich's Psychology of Religion from the Contemporary Perspective

Oesterreich's writings are still up to date when the meaning of dissociative states for religious experience at the personal level are considered. For example, the Australian psychologist John Schumaker (1995) develops in his work *The Corruption of Reality* a dissociative theory of religious experiences, which have an adaptive function of reality. Although without citing Oesterreich, Schumaker regards dissociative experience of trance as a precondition for religious experience and the suggestive acceptance of religious messages. Dissociative states can be induced through rituals, music, dance, psychoactive substances, or monotony (sensoric deprivation), which allow suggestion of religious contents. Therefore, on the one hand, dissociation promotes the deconstruction of the normal psychological reality, whereas on the other hand suggestions make it possible to reconsted religious reality. For Schumaker, illusions and distortions of reality during dissociative states satisfy the basic human need for coping with negative affects caused by reality. Especially religious rituals are trance-supporting and enable the reconstruction of religious realities. Empirical studies have shown that religious rituals are connected to forms of dissociation (Dorahy & Lewis, 2001; Dorahy Schumaker, Krishnamurty, & Kumar, 2001) and depersonalization (Demmrich, Wolfradt, & Domsgen, 2013). However, recent studies (e.g., Breslin & Lewis, 2015) emphasize that dissociation is not a separate precondition for religious experience, but that religious experience "incorporates an element of dissociation" (p. 31).

Many years ago, Traugott Konstantin Oesterreich developed his own conception of psychology of religion based on French psychopathology and German philosophy of value. His conception postulates that nonpathological dissociation is the foundation of religious experience. Whether dissociative states are a precondition or are a part of religious experience can be regarded as an interesting aim for future studies (e.g., Breslin & Lewis, 2015).

References

Belzen, J. A. (2015). *Religionspsychologie: Eine historische Analyse im Spiegel der internationalen Gesellschaft* [Psychology of Religion: A historical analysis in the mirror of the International Society]. Heidelberg: Springer.

Breslin, M. J., & Lewis, C. A. (2015) Dissociation and religiosity: The role of religious experience. *Journal of Spirituality in Mental Health, 1*, 26–33.

Demmrich, S., Wolfradt, U., & Domsgen, M. (2013). Dissociation in religion and spirituality: God images and religious rituals in the context of dissociative experiences among a sample of German adults. *Journal of Empirical Theology, 26*, 229–241.

Dorahy, M. J., & Lewis, C. A. (2001). The relation between dissociation and religiosity: An empirical evaluation of Schumaker's theory. *Journal for the Scientific Study of Religion, 40*, 315–322.

Dorahy, M. J., Schumaker, J. F., Krishnamurty, B., & Kumar, P. (2001). Religious ritual and dissociation in India and Australia. *The Journal of Psychology, 131*, 471–476.

James, W. (1985). *The varieties of religious experience*. Harvard University Press. (Original work published in 1902)

Oesterreich, M. (1954). *Traugott Konstantin Oesterreich. Ich-Forscher und Gottsucher. Lebenswerk und Lebensschicksal* [Traugott Konstantin Oesterreich: Ego-Researcher and God Seeker. Lifework and faith of life]. Stuttgart: Fr. Frommanns.

Oesterreich, T. K. (1906/07). Die Entfremdung der Wahrnehmungswelt und die Depersonalisation in der Psychasthenie [The Estrangement of Perception and the depersonalization in the psychasthenia]. *Journal für Psychologie und Neurologie, 7*, 253–276, *8*, 61–97, 141–174, 220–237, *9*, 15–53.

Oesterreich, T. K. (1910). *Die Phänomenologie des Ich und ihren Grundproblemen* [The Phenomenology of Ego und Its Fundamental Problems]. Leipzig: Barth.

Oesterreich, T. K. (1915). *Die religiöse Erfahrung als philosophisches Problem* [The Religious Experience As a Philosophical Problem]. Berlin: Mittler & Sohn.

Oesterreich, T. K. (1917). *Einführung in die Religionspsychologie als Grundlage für Religionsphilosophie und Religionsgeschichte* [Introduction to the Psychology of Religion As a Foundation for the Philosophy and History of Religion]. Berlin: Mittler & Sohn.

Oesterreich, T. K. (1921). *Die Besessenheit.* Langensalza: Wendt & Klauwell. (English publication: Possession, demoniacal and other, 1923). London: Trench Trübner.

Oesterreich, T. K. (1928). *Die Probleme der Einheit und der Spaltung des Ich* [The Problems of Unitiy and Division of Ego]. Stuttgart: Kohlhammer.

Schumaker, J. F. (1995). *The corruption of reality: A unified theory of religion, hypnosis, and psychopathology*. New York: Promotheus.

Wolfradt, U. (2003). *Depersonalisation. Selbstentfremdung und Realitätsstörung.* [Depersonalization, Self-Estrangement, and Disturbance of Reality]. Köln: Kölner Studien Verlag.

Wolfradt, U. (2006). Pierre Janet und die Depersonalisation [Pierre Janet and Depersonalization). In P. Fiedler (Ed.), *Trauma, Dissoziation, Persönlichkeit. Pierre Janets Beiträge zur modernen Psychiatrie, Psychologie und Psychotherapie* [Trauma, Dissociation, Personality. Pierre Janet's Contributions to Modern Psychiatry, Psychology, and Psychotherapy] (Vol. 1, pp. 180–193). Lengerich: Pabst.

Wolfradt, U. (2010). Die Ich-Theorie nach Traugott Konstantin Oesterreich vor dem Hintergrund der Psychologie Pierre Janets [The Ego-Theory by Traugott Konstantin Oesterreich in the Light of the Psychology of Pierre Janet). In P. Fiedler & G. Heim (Eds.), *Psychotherapie: Vom Automatismus zur Selbstkontrolle. Pierre Janets Beiträge zur modernen Psychiatrie und Psychologie* [Psychotherapy: From Automatism to Self Control. Pierre Janet's Contributions to Modern Psychiatry and Psychology] (Vol. 2, pp. 112–125). Lengerich: Pabst.

Wolfradt, U. (2012). Zwischen Patriotismus und Nationalismus: Felix Krueger und Traugott Konstantin Oesterreich – zwei Biographien im Vergleich [Between Patriotsm and Nationalism: Felix Krueger and Traugott Konstantin Oesterreich – Two Biographies in Comparison]. In T. Herrmann & W. Zeidler (Eds.), *Psychologen in Autoritären Systemen* [Psychologists in Authoritarian Systems] (pp. 95–105). Frankfurt/Main: Lang.

CHAPTER 9

The Discontinuous History of the Psychology of Religion and Its Moving Target

Herman Westerink

Summary

In his new book, Jacob Belzen describes the institutional history of the IAPR in terms of discontinuities and conflicts. This article takes these discontinuities as a starting point for a brief, sketchy reconstruction of some of the fundamental tensions and debates concerning the theoretical approach and subject matter in the history of the psychological study of religion. The article highlights the importance of the interplay between developments in theology and religious studies on the one hand, and the psychology of religion on the other hand, and the implications for shifting agendas as regards psychology of religion's object, aim, topic, methods, and theories. The aim of the article is to show that this interplay not only had a huge impact on the developments in the psychology of religion but also helps us to understand and question current debates, trends, and problems in the field.

Introduction

Writing a text on the history of the psychology of religion is not an easy task. There are several reasons for this. Firstly, there is the problem of the definition of the psychology of religion. Only at first sight the answer to this question seems quite obvious. Psychology of religion is the psychological study of religion, or in other words, it is the study of religion with the use of psychological methods and theories. This answer, however, immediately raises other questions, namely: What is religion? and What do we consider to be psychology or psychological research? (Vandermeersch & Westerink, 2007). A quick look at the history of and publications in the psychology of religion shows that there is hardly any consensus on these questions concerning the object, methodology and theoretical outline of research. This lack of consensus and consistency is closely linked to the fact that among psychologists of religion one traditionally not only finds psychologists but also theologians, psychiatrists, sociologists, philosophers, scholars in the field of religious studies and pedagogics, and

 | DOI 10.1163/9789004322011_010

practitioners working in for example health care (Belzen, 2015). Secondly, there is the problem of the different developments and profiles of the psychology of religion in the various countries and parts of the world. This is not only evident when comparing the history of the psychology of religion in the USA and Europe, but also when examining the European context and the various histories, "traditions", and discourses in the different countries. Thirdly, the institutional history of the psychology of religion is one marked by discontinuity, by decline and re-emergence. The study of the hundred-year history of the International Association for the Psychology of Religion or of the journal *Archiv für Religionspsychologie* (both founded in 1914) merely suggests continuity where there is in fact hardly any (Belzen, 2015).

In this article I want to take this history of discontinuity and lack of consistency and consensus as the starting point. I will neither focus on institutional developments (associations, journals, chairs, and departments) nor on the self-definitions or self-descriptions of the psychology of religion one finds in the most important handbooks (Hood, Hill, & Spilka, 2009; Nelson, 2009; Paloutzian & Park, 2005; Wulff, 1997). I will rather focus on the history of the interplay between developments in theology and religious studies on the one hand, and the psychology of religion on the other hand, and its implications for shifting agendas as regards psychology of religion's object, aim, topic, methods, and theories – the psychology of religion's subject is a moving target. Of course, this history is far too complex to reconstruct in one article. I will limit myself to the task of highlighting the importance of some of the motives, turns and trends that had an impact on the developments in the psychology of religion, and that help us to understand and question current debates, trends and problems in the field.

The Emergence of the Psychology of Religion

The emergence and the composition of the psychology of religion as an identifiable scientific field or discipline in the very late 19th century and early 20th century must first of all be situated in the context of the emergence of psychology – and the human sciences in general – from a variety of (more or less) independent practices and scientific fields. The most important ones are psychiatry, neurology, philosophy, and theology.[1]

1 For the following paragraphs, see also Vandermeersch & Westerink, 2007.

Psychiatry and Neurology

Philippe Pinel is often regarded to be the founding father of modern psychiatry. The unchaining of the madmen of Bicêtre, shortly after the French Revolution, was the act that accompanied this liberation of the madmen from their suffering in a culture dominated by out-dated religious representations on demonic possession and witchcraft as causing madness. A closer look at the writings of Pinel reveals, however, shows that things are not that simple. He was convinced that mental illness was caused by intense and exaggerated psychological affects as evidenced in for example overzealous ambitions, religious fanaticism, or obsessive love. Pinel thus focussed on the positive and negative effects of suggestion and indoctrination by pastors and priests – not on outdated religious representations. The so-called moral treatment of the mentally alienated he developed was in line with this focus: "Moral" (psychological) treatment was all about the right use of the medical doctor's authority influencing the patient's ideas. This concept of moral treatment was in line with moderate pastoral models, and indeed Pinel recognized that he used the same moral principles as many pastors did, who equally opposed the overzealous preaching of discomforting ideas that sometimes provoked insanity. His overall opinion on religion was thus much more nuanced than some later authors suggest (Foucault, 1972; Vandermeersch, 1991).

It was only in the mid-nineteenth century, in the period of the Restoration in France – the period in which the church recovered from the anticlerical atmosphere of the French Revolution and regained new societal influence – that psychiatrists such as Maurice Macario, Alexandre Brierre de Boismont, and notably Louis-Florentin Calmeil started to study past and contemporary demonic possession in relation to mental illness. The concrete occasion for this interest was clearly related to the way the new self-confident Catholicism manifested itself in the public sphere: the sudden rise of Marian apparitions, demonic possessions, miraculous cures, spectacular stigmatics, and visionaries, not only in France but also in other European countries. Some psychiatrists clearly represented an anticlerical perspective on religion arguing that religion inherently lead to pathological formations. Others were interested in psychiatry's contributions to the conceptualization of true (normal) and pathological religiousness, while putting to the fore the societal necessity and utility of religion as foundation for the civil morality. These French psychiatrists – whatever their motives and intentions – soon had a common interest that French neurologists would soon claim to be their territory: the hysteric convulsions. The famous Paris neurologists and known laicist republicans Désiré-Magloire Bourneville and Jean-Martin Charcot were fascinated by the hysteric symptom formations apparent in the lives of stigmatics, demonic possesed, ecstatics, and mystics. For these neurologists the historical data pointed in only one direction: most excessive forms of religiosity could be reinterpreted in terms of hysteria and should therefore be considered pathological (Céard, 1994; Lachapelle, 2011; Vandermeersch & Westerink, 2007; Westerink, 2014).

It was thus in the second half of the nineteenth century that first psychiatrists and then also neurologists sought to reinterpret certain religious phenomena in terms of mental illness, not the least with the aim of legitimating their own institutionalized medical discipline, research, practices, and nosological categories. The importance of these developments in nineteenth-century psychiatry and neurology can hardly be overestimated. This first of all concerns the immediate impact of the discourses in psychiatry and neurology on some of the most important protagonists in the field of the psychology of religion, such as Pierre Janet with his studies on hysteria and dissociation, and Sigmund Freud with his study of religion from the perspective of the psychopathologies. Scholars such as Théodore Flournoy and Carl Gustav Jung can also be situated in this context. On a more fundamental level, psychiatry and neurology determined a much broader agenda than those of individual scholars. As regards religion, the focus was completely on individual religiosity, the way it could be influenced and manipulated, and the danger of excessive and pathological forms – the fundamental question being that of the distinction between normal (healthy) and pathological religiosity.

Less well documented in the psychological literature is the Catholic reaction to the implicit or explicit critique of certain forms of piety and mysticism. In the first decades of the twentieth century we can witness a strong new interest in mysticism and – what is from now on called – spirituality. In search of an alternative approach to French laicist psychiatrists and neurologists, striving also towards an alternative to rigorous dogmatic Neo-Scholasticism and interested in finding a Catholic counterpart for the contemporary protestant interest in religious experience (see below), a variety of Catholic scholars such as George Tyrrell, Frederick von Hügel, Evelynn Underhill, Henri Delacroix, and others started to study mystical and spiritual issues in order to develop their own – in some cases profoundly influential – psychological theories concerning mystical and religious experiences relative to the problematic of obedience and submission to religious authority and church teachings. These and other scholars[2] tried to establish their own psychological views in a precarious context: the increasing anti-modernism of the Catholic Church and the associated dismissal of positivist and evolutionist trends in the human sciences

2 In the early 20th century the psychological study of mysticism is part of a broader trend that includes philosophy (e.g., Blondel) and cultural anthropology (e.g., Lévy-Brühl).

(Kugelmann, 2011; Pizarroso, 2014; Talar, 2009). The Catholic Church's anti-modernism undermined the advancement of psychology of religion in the "Catholic" countries, but did certainly not hinder the further study of mysticism and religious experience in what soon became an influential new area of research: the "scientific" study of spirituality in newly established institutes and schools linked to religious congregations (Bregman, 2014; Hvidt, 2012; Westerink, 2012). These historical developments may seem of little interest for scholars in psychology of religion, however, they are of fundamental importance for understanding the crucial issues (definition, fields of inquiry, sources, etc.) in the current debates on spirituality in its relation to religion (see below). For, it is in this context that we find two fundamental notions that can be traced back to the catholic invention of spirituality: 1) spirituality is the subjective core of religion, and 2) spirituality is an in-depth transformative process aimed at personal spiritual growth and progress.

Philosophy and Theology

For many reasons the first study on the history of the psychology of religion – Hermann Faber's *Das Wesen der Religionspsychologie und ihre Bedeutung für die Dogmatik* ("The Essence of the Psychology of Religion in Its Significance for Dogmatics"), published in 1913 – is a very interesting text. Faber not only provides a comprehensive overview of the emergence of the psychology of religion in the 18th and 19th century, but also systematically discusses fundamental issues such as the discipline's object, aim, and methods, and its significance for dogmatics. Striking about this study is the self-evident manner in which Faber links two traditions together – philosophy and theology – when substantiating his claim that the psychology of religion studies religious phenomena in so far as they are "phenomena in the human soul". More concrete, he refers to religious feelings, needs, religious will and experiences, perceptions and motives (Faber, 1913, pp. 66–71). It were philosophers that founded psychology as the study of the human soul, and it were theologians – and occasionally also philosophers – that had put the issue of religious experience and feelings to the fore (Heine, 2005; Vandermeersch & Westerink, 2007).

The emergence of the psychology of religion is first of all situated in the context of the emergence of psychology as the study of the human soul. It were philosophers such as Wilhelm Wundt in Leipzig, William James at Harvard, and others, who started to implement physiological theory and experimental methods in philosophy, setting up laboratories in order to investigate the issues that in modern philosophy, and certainly in post-Kantian and post-Hegelian philosophy, were key issues: What is perception and how does it work?; What is consciousness?[3] In most cases, the underlying model for the psychological investigation of the soul was Cartesian. The soul was seen as a "thing" that could be investigated as separate from and related to the body. The old Cartesian question thus also returned in the new psychological research: what is the soul and what its relation with the body? The emergence of the psychology of religion is situated in this context of philosophy going experimental with the aim to study the soul and its functions and powers. It was Wundt who in one of his latest writings warned against the "disastrous" effects of what proved to be the predominant trend in the early 20th century: the emancipation of psychology from philosophy. Wundt's critique of this emancipation concerned the danger of disconnecting experimental and empirical research from epistemological, metaphysical and anthropological questions (Wundt, 1913). Wasn't psychology still about the soul, and was not the soul first of all a philosophical issue? In fact, psychologists were shifting attention more and more from the study of the soul to the study of the human behavior that could be more easily investigated through empirical methods. In search of significant and measurable correlations metaphysical and anthropological issues were supposedly of minor importance. Some of the effects of this development can still be witnessed today: the growing theoretical and methodological gap between psychology and the humanities, and the problematic position of psychological theories and perspectives concerning the conceptualization of "the soul" in psychology – phenomenological approaches, psychoanalysis, depth psychology, etc. The emancipation from philosophy, one might say, is still continuing, and with Wundt in mind one might wonder "at what cost".

The emergence of the psychology of religion can be situated in this context, however, with one crucial complicating factor: The most influential and engaged psychologists of religion in the first half of the 20th century were theologians, in particular Protestant theologians. It was these theologians that would determine research agendas and the leading definitions of concepts, topics, and aims. Wundt was a Protestant, and so were many of the first pioneers in the psychology of religion. William James' study of the will to believe and of the religious experiences draws upon philosophical sources (idealism,

---

3 Wundt also had a keen interest in religion. This is particularly manifested in his writing on folk psychology (*Völkerpsychologie*), a field of research that was originally the study of what in German romanticism was called *Volksgeist*, but soon developed into the study of the different mentalities in various cultures and societies including the comparative study of mythology and religion in primitive and advanced cultures. This field of research was also influential in the psychology of religion – one can think of Freud's *Totem and Taboo* for example.

pragmatism, and the writings of Charles Renouvier), but there is also a strong protestant line of thought that can be traced back to, firstly, his own puritan background with its focus on personal faith and conversion, and secondly, the influence of Friedrich Schleiermacher's ideas on the essence of religion as feeling and intuition – one might also say "experience" – and its secondary "non-essential" manifestations such as dogmatics, social organization, pedagogics, metaphysics, and morality (Schleiermacher, 1799/2006). The influence of Schleiermacher can hardly be overestimated when looking at the research agendas of the early psychologists of religion. The crucial point here is not simply Schleiermacher's theological turn to religious experience as such, but on a more fundamental level, the problematization of the relation between individual experience on the one hand and the institutionalized religion (church, teachings) on the other hand. William James and others started to study religious experience as being not inherently linked to social and institutional structures, teachings or morals. Some even went a step further. Oskar Pfister, a Swiss minister, student of Sigmund Freud and a Schleiermacher expert, turns to psychology (psychoanalysis) in order to break away from outdated and antiquarian dogmatics. Gustav Vorbrodt, a German minister and founder of the *Zeitschrift für Religionspsychologie* (1907), was even more radical, arguing that psychology should replace dogmatics as the core discipline in theology (Westerink, 2009). The list can be continued with other names – Georg Wobbermin and his research on the relation between religious experience and revealed religion; Karl Girgensohn and his study of religious experience relative to the formation of values; Girgensohn's student Werner Gruehn's further research on religious values. For all these scholars the fundamental question did not concern the relation between philosophy and psychology, but between psychology of religion and theology, more in particular dogmatics. Faber's nuanced conclusion from his historical and systematic research, in which Schleiermacher, Wundt, James, Vorbrodt, and Pfister are the key figures, is that psychology of religion should describe and investigate actual lived faith and religious experience. Dogmatics should be concerned with the conceptualization of true and normative faith (Faber, 1913). This may seem a simple and clear solution to the problem of the relation between two disciplines. But what if the psychologist of religion raises the question of healthy versus unhealthy religiosity? In fact, this is exactly the question raised by James, Hall, Pfister, Vorbrodt, and others. And suddenly it becomes less obvious and clear at what point psychology of religion itself becomes normative and how (hidden) theological agendas and aims determine psychological research. This problem haunts psychology of religion until the present day.

Schleiermacher's influence and impact can be detected in almost every theological engagement with psychology of religion – in James' experimental and theoretical research, in Pfister's psychoanalytic case studies and theoretical writings, in Wobbermin's empirical research, and also in phenomenological research. Karl Beth, a Viennese theologian and scholar in the phenomenology of religion, who established the *Zeitschrift für Religionspsychologie* in 1928 and founded an institute and an international society for the study of the psychology of religion, together with his wife Marianne Beth (Belzen, 2011) organized an international conference on the psychology of unbelief in 1931 (Noth, 2010; Westerink, 2009). Why this specific topic? Beth was convinced that religion originates from a primal symbiotic feeling of connectedness with and participation in the universe as a meaningful totality – a premise that draws upon Schleiermacher and the writings of the French philosopher and anthropologist Lucien Lévy-Bruhl on mystical participation and primitive mentality.[4] In his major writings, Beth focused his attention not only on the essence of religious experience and man's innate need for connectedness and meaning (Beth, 1927, vii), but also on a typology of religiosity and on the problem of unbelief in modern advanced culture. For the theologian and phenomenologist Beth, the psychology of religion as the study of religious experience and faith should free itself from reductionist and positivist approaches such as developed in Freudian psychoanalysis, and instead highlight man's innate and often unconscious religious cravings. Beth touched upon something important: the relation between religious experience and an underlying often unconscious need or wish for participation in a meaningful universe. Because of Beth's forced emigration to the USA the psychological research on this issue was not continued in Vienna. But the issue was to become important in another part of Europe. Beth's colleague in Groningen, the Dutch theologian and phenomenologist of religion Gerardus van der Leeuw, shared Beth's interests in primitive mentality, meaning and religious experience, and also shared his skepticism about reductionist psychological approaches such as psychoanalysis (e.g., van der Leeuw, 1937). According to Van der Leeuw, all religions "originate from the same functioning of the human mind" and that they can be studied as "a psychological unity" (Van der Leeuw, 1918, p. 5, my translation). Modern man, however, carrying the weight of the Cartesian subject-object-dichotomy, had lost this sense of unity. Phenomenological and psychological approaches could help to regain

4 According to Lévy-Brühl, primitive mentality was prelogic (hence, included the possibility of "logical" contradictions) and mystic, by which he meant the belief in forces and influences that are invisible and yet perceived as real as visible objects and the feeling of unity or "continuum" with the cosmos (Lévy-Brühl, 1910/1922, 1922).

the sensitivity for and understanding of "totality of meaning" as ultimately revealed by God. This expresses a strong theological position and objective in his phenomenological writings (comp. Leertouwer, 1991; Westerink, 2010).

Van der Leeuw's fundamental ideas on phenomenology and psychology were challenged by his student Fokke Sierksma in the 1950s. Sierksma argued that Van der Leeuw's theories and methods were in the risk of being nothing but subjective projections of inner psychic constructions into the outside world. The only way to avoid this risk was the emancipation from the psychology of religion from theology. Instead of a psychology of religion that should support man's innate search for mystic participation and meaning, psychology should focus on the modern subject's own structuring of reality and aim at insight at the subject's illusionary projections of his inner world in the outside world (Sierksma, 1956/1977). Sierksma thus raised fundamental questions regarding the study of religious experience and religious perception. Had the religious experience since the days of Schleiermacher not been too much the final retreat of a theology subjected to a critique of church institutions, dogmatics and religious morality? Was there not a need to finally start raising critical questions about the status of religious experience from a non-theological perspective as well? The reaction came from the catholic priest and psychologist of religion Han Fortmann who wrote a voluminous book in which he argued that theology had a lot to gain from psychotherapy and psychology as auxiliary sciences to re-establish the relation between theology and practice, and that therefore psychology of religion should not be detached from theology (Fortmann, 1964–1968/1981). But what psychology? His book is by and large a defence of the religious experience, and it is a strong critique of all reductionist "projection theories", particularly psychoanalysis. According to Fortmann, Lévy-Bruhl and Van der Leeuw were right when they interpreted participation as the undividedness of subject and world. This is exactly what is lost in religion in the modern secularized world, but what could be rediscovered in religious experience. Modern man has lost contact with his own primitive religious nature through the modern subject-object dichotomy. When Fortmann evaluates the first volume of his study he writes: "Our aim was to save perception, especially the primitive, naive, spontaneous perception. I must admit, that I made this effort in order to save the faith of believers" (Fortman, 1966–1968, Part 1, p. 381, my translation). Contrary to Sierksma, Fortmann proved very influential in the Netherlands, setting the agenda for the next generations of psychologists in religion: the study of religious experience relative to the search for meaning, i.e., meaning making (Westerink, 2009, 2010).

No doubt the psychological research on meaning (meaning making, constructs of meaning) has become an important and interesting part of current psychology of religion. From our short sketch we can see the not self-evident way in which the research on religious experience progressed – from philosophy, via theology to psychology. Much has been gained, but what has been lost? Probably many interesting questions and perspectives that were part of the debates and confrontations between the various approaches and perspectives – empirical and experimental research, phenomenology of religion, psychoanalysis; philosophy, (Protestant and Catholic) theology, psychology. Let me articulate only one striking issue. William James wanted to study religious experiences in its most extreme and intense forms: "We learn most about a thing when we view it under a microscope, as it were, or in its most exaggerated form. This is as true of religious phenomena as of any other kind of fact. The only cases likely to be profitable enough to repay our attention will therefore be cases where the religious spirit is unmistakable and extreme" (James, 1902, p. 39). For other reasons, French psychiatrists and neurologists also focussed their attention on extreme forms of religiosity. Sigmund Freud studied religion as far as it could be analyzed in analogy with psychopathologies. The common idea here is the focus on the extreme, the abnormal, the exaggerated, and therefore also the marginal phenomena that give us the best insight in religious live. Psychological research has moved in the opposite direction. In quantitative empirical research the starting point is not the abnormal but the average: random populations provide the data. Theoretical and empirical research on meaning in general starts from the premise that all individuals give meaning or ask the question for meaning. In short, psychologists no longer study religion "under a microscope" but through a wide-angle lens, as it were. The question is not only what you see and don't see when looking through different lenses, but also what is most interesting to see and what exactly provides us the best understanding of certain forms of religiosity and spirituality. Fact is that the phenomena the earliest psychologists of religion were most interested in – mysticism, conversion, extreme (abnormal and/or pathological) manifestations of religion – have almost disappeared from current psychological research.

From Belief to Spirituality

The 1931 international conference in Vienna had highlighted the importance of the topic of belief and unbelief in the psychological research on religion. Given the theological interest in the relation between lived faith and dogmatics in an age of religion critique and secularization, this topic can hardly be called a surprise. It is impossible and also necessary to provide an encompassing overview of all psychological research on faith, belief and unbelief ranging from Allport's studies on intrinsic and extrinsic motivations, Stark and Glock's five dimension of faith, Fowler's theories on the stages of faith to Wulff's types of religion, and Hutsebaut's post-critical belief scale. What I want to deal with here is linked to the Fortmann quote cited above: In the psychology of religion, faith is at stake. Obviously, Fortmann implicitly admits his apologetic intentions when dismissing reductionist projection theories in favor of a more phenomenological – and theological – approach of religious experience and perception. We should not forget here that from the 1950s onward again, like in the early days of the psychology of religion, many influential psychologists of religion were also clergymen. The main difference: This time Catholics were involved. And it is against this background that we have to raise a question beyond the obvious – the problem of apologetics as such – namely the question of the conceptualization of faith, belief and unbelief relative to individual and social life.

We have seen that in the early psychology of religion many protagonists highlight individual religious experience as "the essence of religion" and as not inherently related to social institutions and dogmatics, and sometimes even as opposed to the latter. One can at least partly understand early 20th century catholic interest in psychology and spirituality as a reaction against this trend: The early sudden engagement with mysticism and what was soon to be called "spirituality" was strongly inspired by a need to think through the relation between what traditionally called *fides qua* and *fides quae,* in short, the relation between the mental act of believing on the one hand and the dogmas and creeds people were supposed to believe and to be committed to on the other hand. In other words, whereas Protestants sometimes tended to criticize dogmatics from the perspective of lived faith, Catholic scholars in spirituality were interested in finding the right interplay between lived individual faith and the social, institutional, and dogmatic space in which this faith is situated. Related to these perspectives is the fundamental anthropological question whether religiosity originates from and in the individual, for example as intense experience or as innate need for meaning, or from the interaction between individual and social sphere – a fundamental anthropological issue since it ultimately concerns the question whether man is naturally *homo religiosus* (or *homo spiritualis*), or not (comp. Belzen, 2010; Stifoss-Hansen, 1999).

The question of the relation between faith and doctrine resp. institutional organizations becomes a contested question from the 1960s onward, that is, in the context of growing awareness of secularization and new radical forms of religion critique. Could the faith of believers really be saved given this cultural climate? In Germany, one of the trailblazers of psychology of religion, the protestant theologian Joachim Scharfenberg (Belzen, 1997), returned to the writings of Pfister and the idea that Freudian psychoanalysis could be used as a *Fremdprophetie* to not only criticize outdated Christian dogmatics resulting, authority structures, and the focus on guilt resulting the neurotization of religion, but also to underscore the aspects of human life essential to religion – love, maturation, sublimation (Westerink, 2009). The "fatherless society" might actually prove to be the fertile soil for a rediscovery of the essential aspects of religion. In the Netherlands, Fortmann conceptualized faith in terms of man's search for coherence of meaning, while strongly drawing upon the theological writings of Romano Guardini on religious experience as the existential experience of the meaning of life beyond the worldly contingencies.

From the 1960s onward Antoine Vergote – a Catholic theologian, philosopher, and psychologist of religion – developed his own influential position in the psychology of religion. In his writings he outs a powerful critique of what he regards the fundamental problem in many psychological theories on man's religiosity, namely the turn to individual needs, motivations and capacities and the tendency to think of religion as originating from or at least naturally corresponding with these psychic aspects. According to Vergote, these theories are highly problematic: The complex and multidimensional phenomenon of religion is reduced here to the mere function of facilitating man's needs, such as the need of meaning (e.g., Belzen, 1998; Vergote, 1997, 2000). Already in his first major book on the psychology of religion, Vergote utters his critique of illusionary and imaginary theoretical constructs that view religion as resulting from primitive mentality and the capacity to connect with the meaningful universe (Vergote, 1970). In other words, he criticizes those scholars that focus on "a religious finality in human nature" for not actually studying religion, but worldviews that originate "in the speculative mind which asks questions about the world as totality" (Vergote & Van der Lans, 1986). But a worldview in which needs and wishes are manifested is not religion. According to Vergote, religion should be seen as unmotivated by innate natural tendencies and capacities, but instead should be regarded as a symbolic system composed of linguistic expressions, emotions, actions and signs that refer to transcendental beings, and that can be recognized as an entity in the cultural realm (Westerink, 2009, p. 217 ff). It is through socialization and the individual's response to revelation that man can enter a symbolic relationship with God or gods that is always more than just a personal relationship but also an entrance into community practice. Notably drawing upon psychoanalytic theory (Freud, Lacan), Vergote thus opposes the psychologist's reductionist and functionalist turn to subjectivity while underscoring the fundamental interplay between individual religiosity and religion as a cultural entity. Religious language is therefore the key to understand religious experience not as a mere subjective feeling, but as a complex symbolic intersubjective process. Whereas others regard the "fatherless society" the ideal opportunity for the emancipation of the subjective essence of religion, Vergote – standing in a more Catholic tradition – argues that such fatherless society, i.e., a society in which intersubjectivity and symbolic functions erode, will merely breed imaginary worldviews.

Behind the psychological conceptualization of faith, belief, and unbelief, we thus find more fundamental position relative to theological standpoints as regards the essence of religion. Despite the powerful critique of certain psychological perspectives on religion, Vergote's own theories strongly depend on the idea that religion is an identifiable cultural entity – identifiable in terms of shared tradition and language, communal forms and practices, shared values and norms. But it is exactly this kind of religion that is rapidly declining in Western secularized culture – not only in Western Europe, but also in the United States. Religion has become more and more a moving target. The spectacular emergence of spirituality as the primal subject of psychological research in the past few decades can be situated in this context. The emergence of the concept of spirituality in the psychology of religion is closely related to the decreasing importance of traditional religious institutions and religiosity as commitment to traditional contents of belief (Ričan, 2004). Notably in American literature on the growing group of people considering themselves spiritual and not religious (e.g., Mercadante, 2014; Streib & Hood, 2011), but increasingly also in European psychology of religion, spirituality is associated with personal life principles and concerned with ultimate questions about life's meaning in relation to or search for the transcendent or sacred (Huguelet & Koenig, 2009; Nelson, 2009; Pargament, 1999; Utsch & Klein, 2011; Westerink, 2013; Zinnbauer & Pargament, 2005). In this context it is hardly a surprise that the study of personal meaning making gains momentum. Israela Silberman for example argues that:

> Individuals operate on the basis of personal beliefs and theories that they have about themselves, about others, about the world of situations they encounter, and their relations to it. These beliefs or theories form idiosyncratic meaning systems that allow individuals to give meaning to the world around them and to their experiences, as well as to set goals, plan activities, and order their behaviour. (Silberman, 2005, p. 644)

Such meaning or belief systems reflect general human needs, such as the need for a coherent personal conceptual system, the need for pleasure and well being in the foreseeable future, the need of self-esteem, and the need of maintenance of good relationships with significant other persons. Such a view can be easily harmonized with existing views on meaning making in Europe, despite the fact of the different intellectual traditions behind these views, because of a strong common trait, namely the distinction between personal spirituality and meaning making on the one hand and religion associated with out-dated dogmatics and institutions on the other hand.

However, things are not that simple. Again, the psychologist's target is a moving target. The reason for this is not only the simple fact that because spirituality is seen as an individual operation of composing one's spiritual beliefs and practices from the contemporary spiritual supermarket – and is therefore never easily identifiable – but, on a more fundamental level, the concept of spirituality itself is highly ambiguous. In the social sciences and religious studies spirituality is mostly associated with the growing individualization and pluralisation of religion since the 1960s. But there is also another important aspect to the discourse on spirituality, namely the very invention and promotion of the term in early 20th century Catholic contexts (see above). In current debates on the concept of spirituality we thus stumble upon on old issue: the felt necessity to reflect faith and religious experience relative to Christian tradition (dogmas, institutions, etc.). Is spirituality the – mystical, experiential – core of the religious tradition and as such manifest in shared religious convictions and practices? Or is spirituality the individual expression of spiritual needs that may be facilitated by religion, but not necessarily so?

Final Remarks

Whatever the answer to the previous questions might be, it can hardly be disputed that psychology of religion is more and more becoming the psychology of spirituality. In a secular age this is surely a transition important for the very future of the psychology of religion itself. After all, in the context of secularization the study of spirituality is a promising field – more promising than the so-called out-dated religious traditions. But this also reasoning has some problematic implications that I can only briefly address here. Currently, we can witness the slow but unmistakable disappearance of classic topics from the psychological research on religion – the psychology of faith, belief and unbelief, the study of religious language, the research on religious and mystical experience, the intersubjective structuring of religious life, the case studies on extreme religious manifestations (mysticism, conversion, etc.) – in favour of research on more broad, diffused, and murky phenomena such as spirituality, well-being, meaning, and existential issues. But is religion really a phenomenon that more and more belongs to the past? The answer depends on one's view on secularization and transformation processes in religion. Any strong distinction between spirituality and religion runs the risk of negating the historical relation between the two and thus of misunderstanding the ways in which religion is transformed and still present in contemporary Western societies. In my opinion, a fundamental issue that deserves more attention is the question what aspects of traditional religion are still – transformed – elements of contemporary worldviews and practices. This presupposes a profound insight in religious traditions and phenomena – and this calls for more interdisciplinary research in which (again) religious studies and theology are important partners. Given psychology of religion's long entanglement with as well as struggle for emancipation from theology, this is not self-evident. After all, the slow transition from the psychology of religion into a psychology of spirituality could be interpreted as the sign or result of this emancipation process itself.

References

Belzen, J. A. (1997). Reflections on the passing away of a trailblazer: Joachim Scharfenberg, 1927–1996. *The International Journal for the Psychology of Religion, 7*, 53–55.

Belzen, J. A. (1998). Religie, zingeving, spiritualiteit: Waar gaat godsdienstpsychologie eigenlijk over? In J. Janssen, M. H. F. van Uden, & H. van der Ven (Eds.), *Schering en inslag. Opstellen over religie in de hedendaagse cultuur* (pp. 207–224). Nijmegen: KSGV.

Belzen, J. A. (2010). *Towards cultural psychology of religion. Principles, approaches, applications*. New York: Springer.

Belzen, J. A. (2011). A political end to a pioneering career: Marianne Beth and the psychology of religion. *Religions, 2*(3), 247–263.

Belzen, J. A. (2015). *Religionspsychologie. Eine historische Analyse im Spiegel der Internationalen Gesellschaft*. Berlin: Springer.

Bregman, L. (2006). Spirituality: A glowing and useful term in search of meaning. *Omega: The Journal of Death and Dying, 53*(1–2), 5–26.

Bregman, L. (2014). *The ecology of spirituality. Meanings, virtues, and practices in a post-religious age*. Waco: Baylor University Press.

Céard, J. (1994). Démonologie et démonopathies au temps de Charcot. *Histoire des Sciences Médicales, 4*, 337–343.

Faber, H. (1913). *Das Wesen der Religionspsychologie und ihre Bedeutung für die Dogmatik*. Tübingen: Mohr.

Fortmann, H. (1964–1968/1981). *Als ziende de Onzienlijke. Een cultuurpsychologische studie over de religieuze waarneming en de zogenaamde religieuze projectie*, I–II, Hilversum: Gooi en Sticht.

Foucault, M. (1972). *Histoire de la folie à l'âge classique*. Paris: Gallimard.

Heine, S. (2005). *Grundlagen der Religionspsychologie. Modelle und Methoden*. Göttingen: Vandenhoeck & Ruprecht.

Hood, R. W., Hill, P. C., & Spilka, B. (2009). *The psychology of religion, fourth edition: An empirical approach*. New York: Guildford Press.

Hvidt, N. C. (2012). Senseless suffering? On the complexity of meaning-making resources. In K. Appel, C. Danz, S. Rosenberg, R. Potz, & A. Walser (Eds.), *Religion in Europa heute: Sozialwissenschaftliche, rechtswissenschaftliche und hermeneutisch-religionsphilosophische Perspektiven* (pp. 173–190). Vienna: Vienna University Press.

James, W. (1902). *The varieties of religious experience*. New York: Longmans, Green and Co.

Kugelmann, R. (2011). *Psychology and Catholicism. Contested boundaries*. Cambridge: Cambridge University Press.

Lachapelle, S. (2011). *Investigating the supernatural: From spiritism & occultism to psychical research & metaphysics*. Baltimore: John Hopkins University Press.

Leertouwer, L. (1991). Primitive religion in Dutch religious studies. *Numen. International Review for the History of Religion, 38*, 198–213.

Lévy-Bruhl, L. (1910/1922). *Les functions mentales dans les sociétés inférieures*. Paris: Alcan.

Lévy-Bruhl, L. (1922). *La mentalité primitive*. Paris: Presses Universitaires de France, 1947.

Mercadante, L. A. (2014). *Belief without borders: Inside the minds of the spiritual but not religious*. Oxford: Oxford University Press.

Nelson, J. M. (2009). *Psychology, religion, and spirituality*. New York: Springer.

Noth, I. (2010). *Freuds bleibende Aktualität: Psychoanalyserezeption in der Pastoral- und Religionspsychologie im deutschen Sprachraum und in der USA*. Stuttgart: Kohlhammer.

Paloutzian, R. F., & Park, C. (Eds.). (2005). *Handbook of the psychology of religion and spirituality*. New York/London: Guildford Press.

Pargament, K. (1999). The psychology of religion and spirituality? Yes and no. *International Journal for the Psychology of Religion*, 9(1), 3–16.

Pizarroso, N. (2014). Henri Delacroix's psychology of religion in context: Between secular religious sciences, William James' psychology and Marcel Mauss' sociology. *International Psychology, Practice and Research, 5*.

Ričan, P. R. (2004). Spirituality: The story of a concept in the psychology of religion. *Archive for the Psychology of Religion, 26*, 135–156.

Schleiermacher, F. D. E. (1799/2006). *On religion. Speeches to its cultural despisers* (R. Crouter, Ed.). Cambridge: Cambridge University Press.

Sierksma, F. (1956/1977). *De religieuze projectie. Een antropologische en psychologische studie over de projectie-verschijnselen in de godsdiensten*. Amsterdam: Meulenhoff.

Silberman, I. (2005). Religion as a meaning system: Implications for the new millenium. *Journal of Social Issues, 61*(4), 641–663.

Stifoss-Hansen, H. (1999). Religion and spirituality: What a European ear hears. *International Journal for the Psychology of Religion, 9*, 25–33.

Streib, H., & Hood, R. W. (2011). "Spirituality" as privatized experience-oriented religion: Empirical and conceptual perspectives. *Implicit Religion, 14*(4), 433–453.

Talar, C. J. T. (Ed.). (2009). *Modernists and mystics*. Washington: The Catholic University of America Press.

Utsch, M., & Klein, C. (2011). Religion, Religiosität, Spiritualität. Bestimmungsversuche für komplexe Begriffe. In C. Klein, H. Berth, & F. Balck (Eds.), *Gesundheit – Religion – Spiritualität. Konzepte, Befunde und Erklärungsansätze* (pp. 25–45). Weinheim: Juventa.

Van der Leeuw, G. (1918). *Plaats en taak van de godsdienstgeschiedenis in de theologische wetenschap*. Groningen: Wolters.

Van der Leeuw, G. (1937). *De primitieve mensch en de religie*. Groningen/Batavia: Wolters.

Vandermeersch, P. (1991). The victory of psychiatry over demonology: The origin of the nineteenth century myth. *History of Psychiatry, 2*, 351–363.

Vandermeersch, P., & Westerink, H. (2007). *Godsdienstpsychologie in cultuurhistorisch perspectief*. Amsterdam: Boom.

Vergote, A. (1970). *Religionspsychologie*. Olten/Freiburg: Walter-Verlag.

Vergote, A. (1997). *Religion, belief and unbelief. A psychological study*. Amsterdam/Atlanta: Leuven University Press.

Vergote, A. (2000). De toekomstige godsdienstpsychologie. Een vooruitzicht. In J. A. Belzen (Ed.), *Op weg naar morgen. Godsdienstpsychologie in Nederland. Teksten II* (pp. 178–193). Kampen: Uitgeverij Kok.

Vergote, A. & Van der Lans, J. (1986). Two opposed viewpoints concerning the object of the psychology of religion. In J. A. Belzen, & J. van der Lans (Eds.), *Current issues in the psychology of religion. Proceedings of the third symposium on the psychology of religion in Europe* (pp. 67–81). Amsterdam: Rodopi.

Westerink, H. (2009). *Controversy and challenge. The reception of Sigmund Freud's psychoanalysis in German and Dutch-speaking theology and religious studies*. Vienna/Berlin: LIT Verlag.

Westerink, H. (2010). Participation and giving ultimate meaning. Exploring the entanglement of psychology of religion and phenomenology of religion in the Netherlands. *Numen. International Review for the History of Religions, 57*(2), 186–211.

Westerink, H. (2012). Spirituality in the psychology of religion: A concept in search of its meaning. *Archive for the Psychology of Religion, 34*(1), 3–15.

Westerink, H. (2013). Religious and spiritual constructs of meaning and transformation. In H. Westerink (Ed.), *Constructs of meaning and religious transformation: Current issues in the psychology of religion* (p. 9–20). Vienna: Vienna University Press.
Westerink, H. (2014). Demonical possession and the historical construction of melancholy and hysteria. *History of Psychiatry, 25*(3), 335–349.
Wulff, D. M. (1997). *Psychology of religion. Classic and contemporary*. New York: Wiley.
Wundt, W. (1913). *Die Psychologie im Kampf ums Dasein*. Leipzig: Alfred Körner Verlag.
Zinnbauer, B. J., & Pargament, K. J. (2005). Religiousness and spirituality. In R. F. Paloutzian & C. Park (Eds.), *Handbook of the psychology of religion and spirituality* (pp. 21–42). New York: Guildford Press.

CHAPTER 10

A Cultural Psychological Reading of *Religionspsychologie*

Tania Zittoun

Summary

Jacob Belzen's *Religionspsychologie* (Belzen, 2015) is a fascinating, deeply scholarly written book retracing a century of psychology of religion in Europe and its relation to the rest of the world. It both shows the anchorage of psychology of religion in the debates taking place around the development of psychology, and in the evolution of Europe since the beginning of the 20th century. In this brief commentary, I highlight the qualities of this work, and especially its ability to retrace the complex human network of relationships that accompanied the development of a scientific society and its publications. I then suggest two possible ways to complement this analysis. First, as a developmental, sociocultural psychologist, I reflect on the fact that this field of enquiry, that aimed to be inter-confessional, came to be led essentially by scholars of Christian origin or addressing Christianity. Second, observing the variety of approaches constituting psychology of religion today, as highlighted by Belzen, I emphasize the diverse epistemologies grounding these works. I finally argue in favor of a pragmatic stance, which might both guide the field into issues of societal relevance, and allow psychology of religion to contribute to the development of psychology as a whole.

Introduction

Jacob Belzen's *Religionspsychologie* (Belzen, 2015) is a fascinating, deeply scholarly written book retracing a century of psychology of religion in Europe and its relation to the rest of the world. Yet paradoxically, it is also a very amusing book – first, because it is led like a conversation with a pleasant interlocutor, eager to share his enthusiasm, and second, because doing the history of a research field – not to say a discipline – Belzen also retraces the history of a century, of psychology, and mostly, the stories of many intermeshed lives – masters and disciples, husbands and wives, admirers and enviers, mystical and empiricists. To this century-broad fresco of human passion and intelligence, there is not much to add. I will simply make a comment on the first

 | DOI 10.1163/9789004322011_011

sections of the book, and address a more prospective point related to the third section.

A Not-So Ecumenical Science of Religion

One of my recent surprises as I attended a few meetings of psychologists dealing with religious issues, which I found reflected in the first two sections of the book, is how much the psychology of religion has long been mainly a Christian project in Europe. It is also what appears to be the case in the almost hundred years of the International Association for the Psychology of Religion, the *Internationale Gesellschaft,* and the publication that would become the *Archive for the Psychology of Religion.* Although there has been explicit an intention to promote inter-confessional debates and to overcome religious differences when the society was created at the beginning of the 20th century in Germany, it actually seems that for most of the society's existence, these inter-confessional issues mainly concerned various forms of Catholicism, reformed churches, and Protestantism (Belzen, 2015, Chapter 4). Of course, some "religious-free" or trans-religious questions were raised by the members of the society – about belief or mysticism, for instance – and some others were also raised about civilization distant in time and space, in a perspective closer to Wundt's *Völkerpsychologie.* Yet most involved authors in Europe were also attracted to psychology of religion in link to their own religious origin or orientation, claimed, or problematic – which were all Christian. This seems to have changed only with the entry on the stage of the International Association of the provoking Ms. Marianne Beth, a scholar who was both the first woman involved, as well as the first participant of Jewish origin – although her interest was not oriented toward Judaism. The fact of her religious origin, mentioned by Belzen in the context of the uprising of the National-Sozialismus (Belzen, 2015, p. 102), is however not further developed – a discretion which can be understood – yet one may wonder about this. Interestingly, Beth also engaged dialogue with the Kant-Gesellschaft, which grouped many Jewish intellectuals (Martin Buber, Hannah Arendt, Georg Simmel, etc.). This society was mainly a philosophical one, yet interested in questions related to the psychology of religion (Belzen, 2015, p. 93). Why were these authors not more closely associated to the project of the *society* is however not addressed further. Aware that I miss much information here, and also, wanting to avoid any essentialization on the basis of this observation, I would like to raise a few questions from a theoretical perspective.

From an anthropological or a cultural psychological perspective, any religion is a cultural system, with its rules, norms, taboos, wardens, and epistemic principles, itself located in a given sociocultural environment where it is related to other systems (Dahinden & Zittoun, 2013; Geertz, 1972; Zittoun, 2013a, 2013b). From a developmental perspective, it then follows that a given person, with his or her specific trajectory in the world, exposed to these others, with their discourses, ways of doing, ways of speaking, internalizes and appropriates certain ways of seeing the world, and how through these many things that constitute her, he or she makes an unique sense of herself, others and the world. From such a perspective, if a person developed within a given religious system, that system and people with whom she interacts may facilitate some ways of thinking or acting, guide towards some, or limit others. Hence, various cultural elements – religious or others – progressively can be used as resources for her development, or at times, can become a rather limiting and constraining semiotic guidance (Lawrence, Benedikt, & Valsiner, 1992; Zittoun, 2006a).

Hence, given the fact that most researchers active in the domain of psychology of religion had some personal relations to their religion, as suggests Belzen, then it might be likely that these systems guided their questioning. In that sense, it might interesting to examine how a given religious systems, with its constitutional conditions, supports or prevents certain questions raised by people about the nature of their religious experience or their belonging. Hence, can these questions be formulated within the language of the system itself? Or does it need to draw on other semiotic resources, such as a scientific vocabulary, psychological or philosophical, to address them? Does the fact of using a language or a mode of questioning intrinsic, or external to the religious system, has any other consequences, and for whom? For instance, is it socially more recognized to adopt an academic – philosophical or psychological – rather than a religious language, does it allow to turn such questioning into a more respected one? Reversely, is trying to answer questions about faith or religious experience within the system itself – e.g., though biblical or Midrashic interpretation – an opportunity or a limiting condition, due to the constraining modalities of that system (Baucal & Zittoun, 2013; Zittoun, 2013a)? Or otherwise, is it simply dynamics of inclusion and exclusion, supported by other social networks and belonging, that allowed some researchers to become members of certain groups rather than others?

In his historical analysis, Jacob Belzen is very careful to give space to all orientations and sensibilities present within the field developed as psychology of religion around the International Association and the *Archive*. As an outsider, however, I can only observe this absence of consideration of the primarily Christian rooting of the society, as well as a primary interest for Christian religion in the *Archive*, and I only wonder how much examining this blind sport could enrich or complete the analysis.

And a More Selective Future for Psychology of Religion

Raising this first point, I actually position myself within the very ecumenical panorama of the heterogeneity of psychology of religions, or of relationships between psychology and religion, reviewed by Belzen in the third part of his book (Belzen, 2015, Chapter 11). Although there is a window variety in the objects, used theories, methods, and grounding in current practices of psychology of religion, can we not identify lines of strength, potential for future developments? And if so, how to do so?

As Belzen says, there *is* a psychology of religion, undoubtedly – but why bother, and why still bother now? In my view, the future of psychology of psychology of religion lies not only in the subjective interests of researchers to these matters or to the service of a growing community, but to its social relevance. And to address that issue in a grounded way, we need to turn back to what appears as one absent of the reviews of the pluralisms of psychology of religion today, which is, the plurality of their *epistemological groundings*. In effect, one of the reasons of the apparent eclectism of the approaches identified by Belzen is that these are grounded into very different types of epistemologies. Choosing to evaluate the outcome or church attendance through a questionnaire to address coping mechanism, or studying religious sense-making through a case study (Lawrence et al., 1992) do not only convoke two data gathering techniques (e.g., questionnaires vs. interviews), and two theoretical frames (e.g., medical-positivistic vs. dialogical), they also rely on deeply contrasting conceptions of the nature of social-scientific knowledge, the modalities of its constitution and its outcomes – that is, different epistemologies – from the most naïve realism to postmodern constructivist.

Here, I would like to argue in favor of a pragmatic epistemology to the psychology of religion – a pragmatist stance also adopted by William James (Brandt & Fournier, 2007; James, 1902, 1904b; Zittoun, 2013b), and rejected by some of the early promoters of the International Association (Belzen, 2015, Chapter 3). A pragmatic epistemology encourages studying issues or concepts in such a way that their use makes a difference; either they allow to change one's outlook upon the world, or they allow to act upon it. This can be understood at two levels: that of producing concepts that matter in this double sense, or also, to focus on issues that actually are important for people in themselves (Cornish & Gillespie, 2009; James, 1904a, 1904b). In addition, it encourages a strong and reflexive dialogue between theorization and facts, also called abduction – where neither science should be the flat application of models or theories, nor the pure account of facts, but emerge out of a permanent and mutual enrichment of these two aspects (Zittoun, 2015).

From such a perspective, a few implications can be drawn. First, a useful starting point for a study of psychology of religion is that of issues that do matter for people we – as researchers – study, or with whom we collaborate. Of course, this can be very local. Why do the children of a religious school feel in danger when they venture in the surrounding streets in time of peace (Zittoun, 1996)? Why do University students draw on biblical stories when they move away from home (Zittoun, 2006b)? But it can also take much wider proportions: Why does a whole minority community who used to self-define herself through her national origin or her regional roots, starts to present herself as a religious minority, as the former-Yugoslavs from Switzerland, who then were presented as Kosovars, then Albanese from Kosovo, before becoming "Muslims", in a country which itself starts to fear its religious minorities (Dahinden, Duemmler, & Moret, 2011; Dahinden & Zittoun, 2013; Holtz, Dahinden, & Wagner, 2013)?

In that respect, it might be useful to resituate these dynamics in their wider social and political contexts. Hence, although the march of history is very much present in the background of Belzen's analysis, the analysis of its role in the appearance and disappearance of certain questions could be interesting. The beginning of psychology of religion met the young 20th century, with all the richness diversity in a mainly Judeo-Christian Europe, at a point of relative peace (the large religious wars are over, the troubles in the middle east are far, and the upcoming war is still to manifest itself). Yet two world wars obviously affected psychology of religion – not only because it slowed down publications, and sent to the front or deported some of their authors; indeed, many ferocious proponents simply seem to have lost interest in these questions as more urgent social and political issues were calling them. In the second decade of the 21st century, the cultural and religious landscape is slightly different. Although Europe is still a relatively peaceful patchwork of languages and modes of living, the presence of Islam has radically increased in formerly dominantly Christian areas, in a world context where aggressive fundamentalist groups render the religion's name daily salient in the media. It is in that context that we should question how and why people mobilize their faith, claim a belonging, or why others ostracize specific religious groups. What is it that religions or religious claims or ideas or identities make people do, and what for? Why is "religion" that puts people so much on the move? These questions are pragmatists in a first sense: These are about how specific semiotic systems shape people's gaze on the world and guide their action. This could also become pragmatist in a second sense – how could a psychology of religion allow us to understand, if not prevent dramas, such as the terrorist attacks in most of European capitals or on holiday resorts these past years? How can we produce knowledge that can guide policy makers and practitioners, so as to facilitate peaceful coexistence and mutual understanding in schools and in the workplace?

From a more theoretical stance, we can now also reflect on the development – or absence of development, as suggested by many authors quoted by Belzen – of psychology of religion from a pragmatist perspective. One core question is indeed: To what type or body of knowledge wants psychology of religion to contribute *primarily*? Here Belzen also recalls that there are many ways to consider the links between religion and psychology. As a psychologist within the social sciences, I will reply from my disciplinary perspective. For me, our enquiry should, whatever objects or shapes it takes, contribute to our understanding of people's lives in a changing world. A good observation is thus one that challenges existing theories, and allows developing more powerful or precise understandings of the world. On the one side, psychology of religion, is, to the same extent that a psychology of cooking or playing tennis, a psychology applied to a specific domain of human activity and which allows to understand humans better. Of course, religion as such is not as anodyne as playing tennis – only the former pushed people to cross oceans or deserts, allowed the most delightful human experiences, and justified the slaughters of billions of others. Hence, on the other side, the specific contribution of psychology of religion to psychology and the social sciences as a whole is that it precisely groups a very wide range of human experiences – some very specific, some much less – but unique in their combination (de Rosny, 1981; Hüwelmeier, 2011; James, 1906; Obeyesekere, 2012). In that sense, it actually challenges any theory of psychology – is it strong enough, integrative enough, rich enough to account for these specifically religious phenomena? Some authors have worked in that direction, measuring and advancing their models in the light of religious issues (Erikson, 1993; Freud, 1913; Valsiner, 1998). Although their projects were not formally part of a psychology of religion as an institutional field, they actually participated to its internal debates. Reversely, many simple applications of preexisting conceptual tools from psychology into issues of religion bring very little to theoretical discussions – showing how this or that declared faith is related to self-esteem, gender identification or coping mechanism – and definitely fail to account for the specificity of the psychological phenomena related to religion.

As Belzen beautifully shows, the origins of psychology of religion were deeply rooted to the birth of psychology and its first institutionalization, in Germany around Wundt's laboratory, and in the USA around Hall's work. Some of the structuring problems and debates of the field reflect these wider scientific evolutions, themselves very specifically located in a time and space, allowing exchanges, fostering collaborations and exclusions. Perhaps what psychology of religion has lost by establishing itself as self-standing discipline is its anchorage in wider and foundational debates in psychology, as it once was the case.

To Conclude

My two lines of interrogation are only mosquito mumbles in front of the remarkable historical reconstruction of one century of European academic psychology of religion. As a sociocultural psychologist, thanks to Jacob Belzen's case study of the development of psychology of religion, I both learned about the development of psychology as a field, and also, about the dynamics of creating scientific societies, about collaborations and rivalries – about the daily activities of social sciences. In both senses, this history of psychology of religion is an invitation to examine the blind spots of psychology as a whole. Also, in turn, I hope that these few lines may also suggest some questions to the blind spots of psychology of religion.

References

Baucal, A., & Zittoun, T. (2013). Religion as dialogical resource: A socio-cultural approach. *Integrative Psychological and Behavioral Science, 47*(2), 207–219 <http://doi.org/10.1007/s12124-013-9229-z>.

Belzen, J. A. (2015). *Religionpsychologie. Eine historische Analyse im Spiegel der Internationalen Gesellschaft*. Berlin, Heidelberg: Springer.

Brandt, P.-Y., & Fournier, C.-A. (Eds.). (2007). *Fonctions psychologiques du religieux : Cent ans après Varieties de William James*. Genève: Labor et Fides.

Cornish, F., & Gillespie, A. (2009). A pragmatist approach to the problem of knowledge in health psychology. *Journal of Health Psychology, 14*(6), 800–809.

Dahinden, J., Duemmler, K., & Moret, J. (2011). *Ethnizität und Religion. Welche Praktiken, Identitäten und Grenzziehungen? Eine Untersuchung mit jungen Erwachsenen. Schlussbericht* (Final report). Neuchâtel & Bern. Retrieved from <http://www.nfp58.ch/files/downloads/Schlussbericht_DahindenJanine.pdf>

Dahinden, J., & Zittoun, T. (2013). Religion in meaning making and boundary work: Theoretical explorations. *Integrative Psychological and Behavioral Science, 47*(2), 185–206 <http://doi.org/10.1007/s12124-013-9233-3>.

de Rosny, E. (1981). *Les yeux de ma chèvre*. Paris: Plon.

Erikson, E. H. (1993). *Young man Luther: A study in psychoanalysis and history*. New York: W. W. Norton & Company.

Freud, S. (1913). *Totem and taboo and other works* (J. Strachey, Ed.) (Vol. 13). London: Karnac Books.

Geertz, C. (1972). La religion comme système culturel. In R. Bradbury, C. Geertz, M. E. Spiro, V. W. Turner, & E. H. Winter (Eds.), *Essais d'anthropologie religieuse* (pp. 19–66). Paris: Gallimard.

Holtz, P., Dahinden, J., & Wagner, W. (2013). German Muslims and the 'integration debate': Negotiating identities in the face of discrimination. *Integrative Psychological and Behavioral Science, 47*(2), 231–248 <http://doi.org/10.1007/s12124-012-9227-6>.

Hüwelmeier, G. (2011). Socialist cosmopolitanism meets global Pentecostalism: Charismatic Christianity among Vietnamese migrants after the fall of the Berlin Wall. *Ethnic and Racial Studies, 34*(3), 436–453 <http://doi.org/10.1080/01419870.2011.535547>.

James, W. (1902). *The varieties of religious experience*. Cambridge, MA: Harvard University Press.

James, W. (1904a). The pragmatic method. *The Journal of Philosophy, Psychology and Scientific Methods, 1*(25), 673–687 <http://doi.org/10.2307/2012198>.

James, W. (1904b). What is pragmatism. In *A new name for some old ways of thinking*. The Library of Amercia. Retrieved from <http://www.marxists.org/reference/subject/philosophy/works/us/james.htm>.

James, W. (1906). *L'expérience religieuse : Essai de psychologie descriptive*. (F. Abauzit, Trans.). Paris/Genève: Felix Alcan/Henry Kündig.

Lawrence, J. A., Benedikt, R., & Valsiner, J. (1992). Homeless in the mind: A case-history of personal life in and out of a close orthodox community. *Journal of Social Distres and the Homeless, 1*(2), 157–176.

Obeyesekere, G. (2012). *The awakened ones: Phenomenology of visionary experience*. New York: Columbia University Press.

Valsiner, J. (1998). *The guided mind: A sociogenetic approach to personality*. Cambridge, MA: Harvard University Press.

Zittoun, T. (1996). Non sono tutti fascisti. Immagini di sé e degli altri nei ragazzi della scuola ebraica. *La Rassegna Mensile Di Israel, 62*(3), 155–187.

Zittoun, T. (2006a). Difficult secularity: Talmud as symbolic resource. *Outlines. Critical Social Studies, 8*(2), 59–75.

Zittoun, T. (2006b). *Transitions. Development through symbolic resources*. Greenwich (CT): Information Age Publishing.

Zittoun, T. (2013a). Religious traditions as means of innovation: The use of symbolic resources in the life course. In H. Zock & M. Buitelaar (Eds.), *Religious voices in self-*

narratives making sense of life in times of transitions (pp. 129–148). Berlin: Walter de Gruyter.

Zittoun, T. (2013b). Une psychologie socioculturelle de l'expérience religieuse : L'exemple du Judaïsme. In P.-Y. Brandt & J. M. Day (Eds.), *Psychologie du développement religieux. Questions classiques et perspectives contemporaines* (pp. 221–248). Genève: Labor et Fides.

Zittoun, T. (2015). Compatibility between early psychoanalysis and pragmatism. In P. J. Rosenbaum (Ed.), *Making our ideas clear: Pragmatism in psychoanalysis* (pp. 23–42). Charlotte, NC: Information Age Publisihing.

CHAPTER 11

Discussing Misunderstanding and Disagreement: Some Responses to Some Readers of a History of the International Association for the Psychology of Religion

Jacob A. Belzen

Summary

This chapter supplies a response to some of the comments in the previous chapters, especially to some misunderstandings, criticisms, and controversies.

Introduction

It is a not too common experience for an author to have an opportunity to discuss in public, even in publications, with some of her or his readers. Many scholars publish their work, oftentimes hardly getting any response at all, perhaps receiving some polite acknowledgement, but no reaction to the content of their thoughts. Therefore, it is a real privilege to have a number of excellent colleagues commenting on a recent study published on what I think are some foundational issues in the psychology of religion, a study for which I took the history of the International Association for the Psychology of Religion (IAPR) as an empirical starting point (Belzen, 2015). Having contributions from authors with different expertise and coming from different countries has allowed for a variety of voices and perspectives, which certainly has resulted in a fine *bouquet* being presented to IAPR and *Archive*, both now on their way into their second century. But a large disadvantage also needs to be mentioned: There is no contribution from the USA, which is, without doubt, the country, or rather the continent, where the largest part of publications in present psychology of religion is produced. This is a real shortcoming, for which the reason is simple, however: almost none of the many psychologists of religion over there is still able to read a text in German, the language in which *Religionspsychologie*, based as its historical middle part is on mainly sources in German, is written. (And among the American historians of psychology, who oftentimes are still

 | DOI 10.1163/9789004322011_012

able to read German, almost no one is acquainted enough with the psychology of religion to dare enter a discussion of it.[1]) Nevertheless, we have a sufficiently large number of issues put on the table. Our esteemed colleagues have reacted to *Religionspsychologie* in quite diverse ways: Some have been inspired to add to our knowledge of history by treating an oeuvre that fell out of the scope of the book, some were prompted to share a number of reflections on the field, and some have articulated problems with or at least questions about *Religionspsychologie* itself. Unfortunately, in the following, I cannot deal exhaustively with all the issues brought up; and not entering into discussion about this or that in the antecedent papers does therefore not express disinterest or disagreement on my part, but simply lack of space.

What and Whom to (Not) Study and for What Reasons?

As trivial as it sounds, the opening sentence of Westerink's contribution to this special issue on the history of the psychology is religion is true enough: Writing a text on the history of the psychology of religion is not an easy task. It is not an impossible task, however, for a number of texts do exist that deal with the topic mentioned. These texts are of very different kinds and quality and they all have their own problems. For briefness sake, one could categorize these historicizing texts loosely into (1) such that offer, more or less eclectically, an *ensemble* of names and/or theories from the past, (2) such that introduce into an author's point of view, and (3) such that bear the characteristics of scholarly work in a narrow sense. In the first type of work, well-read authors, like recently Heine (2005) or Vandermeersch and Westerink (2007), usually discuss a number of works from the past, but a problem with this type of work is almost always that it is not clear why the author discusses A and D from the past, but leaves out B and C. In the second type of work, there is the danger of some distortion of the viewpoints chosen for discussion, as they figure in a presentation of the author's own theory, a theory usually aiming to overcome the imperfections in the theories presented. Important works like the ones by Vergote (1966/1967, 1984/1997) almost inevitably are insufficiently treating opinions of others. While in-depth treatises of a certain oeuvre, the third type of work (of which

1 The obvious exception here is David M. Wulff, who is widely read in and well acquainted with past and present psychology of religion in Europe and for years a leader of the field in the USA. He would have been in the best position to comment on a study on IAPR. Right from the beginning, he has been involved in the present project, but for personal reasons he unfortunately had to withdraw.

dissertations like Klünker [1985] or Machoń [2005] present examples) is often very limited in scope, as it discusses only this or that oeuvre. Obviously, all types have their virtues too, among which should be mentioned, especially with the third type, the combination of modesty and precision so characteristic of real scholarly work: Contrary to what many, especially outside the academic world, think, science does not claim to know everything. Science only provides a very special kind of knowledge (it does neither provide all knowledge nor embracing knowledge); while precise about what was investigated about something specific (X), science does not even claim to know everything about X.

Occasioned as *Religionspsychologie* was by the centenary of the International Association for the Psychology of Religion (IAPR) and its publication medium, the choice to deal with the history of that association seemed to be an obvious choice, yet it is a choice that implies shortcomings too. While the choice for IAPR and its international context provides a clear scope and the advantages of both remaining systematic in empirical research and manageable in amount of work to be dealt with, it necessarily disregards or mentions only in passing all kinds of persons, events and developments that a more comprehensive history of the psychology of religion would require.[2] IAPR having started as a very central-European (even German only) enterprise, *Religionspsychologie* hardly discusses the without doubt equally interesting beginnings of the psychology of religion in France and in the United States of America. Even worse, given the language barrier, there has been no exploration at all of potential developments in smaller countries like Portugal or Rumania. (The author being Dutch, other small countries like Belgium and The Netherlands did receive at least some attention.) And as discussed at length in *Religionspsychologie* itself, even the "claim" of IAPR being now over one century old, is problematic: IAPR did not really "exist" during all the past hundred years. As a project, the book shares the problems mentioned with some others and hopefully also some of their virtues: It combines a fairly rigid empirical investigation of its object of research in the narrow sense (i.e., IAPR's past) with a fairly lengthy exposé of some of the problems and characteristics of the psychology of religion in a more general sense, both in its past and present.

---

2 Therefore, Norager (this volume) is very correct in adding "hitherto" to his qualifying the book as the "most comprehensive account of European psychology of religion": While it may be true that there is no more comprehensive account, it for sure is *not* an effort to be an account of all of European psychology; the claim, in the empirical part B of the book, is only to provide more and new knowledge about IAPR's past.

It is to be applauded, therefore, that this volume brings some additions to *Religionspsychologie*. Scholars like Oesterreich and Vergote do not really figure in the book, as they were not central to IAPR's past. To remain precise: Although Wolfradt and Demmrich (this volume) state that Traugott Konstantin Oesterreich (1880–1949) has not been a member of IAPR, they do not provide empirical evidence for their claim. (It could well be suspected that he did belong to the very first some hundred people that expressed in 1914 or shortly thereafter their will to join. As there is no IAPR-archive, we just don't know who these people were.) Antoon Vergote (1921–2013) has had considerable impact in the psychology of religion, even far beyond Europe, but his involvement with IAPR was rather marginal (and as a result of his criticism of the organization's tendency, his rare remarks on it were somewhat biased[3]). If one were to study the international organization of the field as such or if one were to discuss the implications of European psychology gradually giving in to being dominated by US-American psychology, Vergote's work would present a fine case-study of not only a complex oeuvre, but also of a complex state of affairs in the psychology of religion. Despite the widely acknowledged high quality of his work, Vergote did not establish a "school" in the usual sense of that word: He did not formulate a specific psychological theory of his own about religion that would have been employed and corroborated by any number of followers (or even adepts). While true, this observation needs to be nuanced immediately too.

First of all, during decades Vergote has had enormous impact on a large number of psychologists of religion, not so much by imposing any theory of his own, but by his way of thinking and theorizing. As lined out very well by Corveleyn (this volume), Vergote employed a very broad, interdisciplinary perspective in the psychology of religion, offering methodological reflection of exceptional depth. His way of doing psychology of religion has not only been a major inspiration to his wide readership, but he himself presented a model of how to be a sophisticated scholar. He probably supervised the highest number of doctoral dissertations in post-war Europe in empirical psychology of religion (next to a much larger number of dissertations in other fields!). In many ways, his work was an expression of the kind of man he was: Like an artist, he did not produce a theory that others could apply, but he offered inspiration (and confrontation!). He did not insist that students would do as he did, but he provided a model of how set out to find an authentic way of pursuing academic interests (whether in psychology, philosophy or theology). Many have

3 In his publication on the future of the psychology of religion (Vergote, 2000), the very critical sentences on IAPR before the 2001-reorganization were only tempered in response to a suggestion of the editor of the volume.

taken up topics, ideas, theories (and sometimes even prejudices...) from him (examples would be the study of god-images, the necessity of a developmental perspective in psychology, the role of unconscious processes and of embodiment, the awareness of the limits of psychology of religion, or even the way he disliked the work by Jung and the way that author was adored by many interested in psychology of religion).

A second reason for Vergote's not establishing a school in the narrow sense of that word is his disinterest of engaging in the kind of political and organizational work (including manipulation) that is usually found in the fabric of any school. Thirdly, he did not devise instruments or techniques that could be easily learned to quickly apply by students and that he would have required using in theses under his supervision. (He did develop empirical techniques that been employed in a number of empirical investigations, but he never insisted others would employ them.) To go short, he did not "use" his students and collaborators, leaving freedom (which is usually more difficult to handle than an empirical technique ...).

A fourth reason was no doubt his not joining the increasing orientation of European psychology, especially in countries with small languages, towards the US-psychology. Although he has been a visiting professor in the USA, he did not only ever try to become really fluent in pronouncing and writing American English (being native Flemish himself, he enjoyed thinking, writing, and talking French), but he also remained skeptical about the Americanization of much of European thought including psychology. His continental way of phrasing was hard to translate into English, which deprived him of a readership in the USA that was steadily increasing. (Without doubt, his work was acknowledged as important by colleagues in the USA, but hardly understood, not only because of the language-barrier, but mainly because of the very different style he employed; just compare the way an oeuvre like Heidegger's, according to many Europeans the most important philosophy of the twentieth century, is still largely neglected in the USA, or compare how fundamentally ill understood many Freudians concepts are over there – according to people like Lacan, and also to Vergote.)

Finally, a factor certainly has been Vergote's remaining faithful to a classical academic approach that reminds many present day psychologists, also in Europe, of philosophy. He took great pain to understand and explicate the meaning of words and notions found with great authors, concentrating on fundamental questions, writing in a dense way, rather than producing short sentences that could easily be understood by anyone with high school education. Especially in his publications on psychoanalysis, his way of discussing concepts reminds more of exegesis (which was a field in which he earned a doctorate before he turned to psychology) than of the present day preference for operationalization, quantification, and statistical analysis that has come to dominate research papers in psychology. (To safeguard against any misunderstanding: Vergote also gave advices like "if you can measure anything, do it!" as a way of doing empirical research, but he never set out to choose *only* this way to work and publish.)

Admittedly a giant in the field, Vergote has nevertheless not been the object of research of *Religionspsychologie*. And he is not the only European to have been largely neglected in the book: As Carl Girgensohn (1875–1925) had been the teacher of Werner Gruehn (1887–1961), who has dominated so much of IAPR's first fifty year, he gets at least a certain amount of attention in the book. But it would be fascinating study to explicate what exactly psychology of religion stood for a with Girgensohn. Girgensohn's fame in the interbellum was derived from his employing the "experimental method" around 1900 to religion, an "experimental method" that was utterly different from what that phrase means at present. Indeed, a study on the employment of the word "experimental" in psychology as such would be fascinating and teach a great deal about how things have evolved in psychology, whether in its variant of psychology of religion, or not. Moreover, it would be highly instructive to see what the role of psychology has been in the larger oeuvre by Girgensohn. (One might well expect it to have been more instrumental than has been acknowledged so far, as some of the remarks by Nørager [this volume] imply.)

It can only be hoped that the publication of a study of a *part* (and only a part!) of the field's past like in *Religionspsychologie* will inspire others to take up other parts of that past and set out for similar investigations, whether of oeuvres, organizations or events.

Modesty being one of the central virtues of all scholarly work, the expectations about *Religionspsychologie* as a publication are only modest too. As pointed out in the book itself, it will probably not be able to correct the prevailing view that "the" psychology of religion would have originated in the United States of America. As has been pointed out by Wulff (1991) decades ago already, as far as we know, there was a more or less simultaneous start in English, French, and German speaking countries, but – depending of course on the definition of what counts as psychology of religion and what does not! – early European "experts on the psyche"[4] like Fechner, Ideler or Pinel clearly had

4 On purpose, I choose a somewhat clumsy circumscription to hint at a group of scholars nowadays often referred to psychiatrists, psychologists, and psychotherapists. While the group certainly includes other professionals with good knowledge of (some aspects of) the psyche and working with psychological aspects of human beings (like counselors of many kinds, but

some kind of professional psychological views about religion and may equally count as early psychologists of religion. Strangely enough, even an excellent reader like Nørager (this volume), however, persists in presenting psychology of religion as being the result of "impulses coming from the USA". An author can be happy if he has achieved a result as reported by Nestler (this volume): Reading *Religionspsychologie*, he came to new and better appreciation of the person and work of Wilhelm Stählin (1883–1975), IAPR's founder, who had been the subject of Nestler's doctoral dissertation (Nestler, 1986).[5]

Wrangling with Wundt

A bit more serious, perhaps, is what seems to be a controversy with Allolio-Näcke (this volume). Voiced by an author with a similar background, Allolio-Näcke's stand is puzzling: He refuses to accept Wilhelm Wundt (1832–1920) as an early psychologist of religion. His argumentation is not convincing, however, and, worse, seems to be unfair to Wundt. Allolio-Näcke's arguments in the main are: Wundt's effort to develop a cultural psychology of religion did not achieve much, Wundt did not cite cultural psychological, but historical studies of religion. The first argument seems to be thoroughly anachronistic: From a contemporary perspective, it may seem that earlier work in psychology (or in whatever scholarly field) is of a poorer quality than contemporary work. But in historical scholarship (as we are involved in with a project on [a part of] the history of the psychology of religion) it is regarded as a fundamental flaw to judge on earlier work by the standards of present work. This flaw is called by names like presentism or hodiecentrism. In contemporary history of science, it is a truism that earlier work should be judged in its own right and be understood from its historical context. (E.g., present day mathematics and physics employing different theories than formulated by Sir Isaac Newton [1643–1727], does not imply that Newton was not a mathematician and physicist!) Whatever the value was, by present or future standards, of Wundt's work in or on the psychology of religion, it is clearly anachronistic to deny him

also many pastors), we should remember that "professions" (complete with educational tracks, diploma's, union-like organizations etc.) like "psychiatrist" did not exist before the twentieth century (and during that century, the "profession" of psychologist was born in different countries in different years).

5 And to immediately temper pride: Both Nestler (this volume) and Nørager (this volume) continue to talk about "the Dorpat School", although *Religionspsychologie* tries to show that such a school never really existed in psychology of religion (it was a phrase mainly instrumental to the private aspirations of Werner Gruehn, IAPR's first secretary-general).

having been a psychologist of religion. Moreover, in all major reviews of European psychology of religion before World War II, Wundt is mentioned as a key figure in the psychology of religion!

That Wundt did not cite many other psychologists of religion but mostly historians of religion, did not make him himself a historian of religion. (It does not seem that Wundt himself ever conducted any actual empirical historical research on religion.) For sure, quite a number of psychologists cite historians, but that does not make them historians. Moreover, Wundt's approach in reviewing (granted: at length) historical and anthropological studies was a psychological one; his principles for analyses were psychological. (Of course, one can doubt the validity and value of the principles he employed, but that is an entirely different issue.) And to remain historically fair: There was not much to quote from psychology of religion in Wundt's days, especially not from a cultural psychological perspective as he wanted to employ in the psychology of religion.

Worst of all, by reasoning as he does, Allolio-Näcke fails to see the innovative importance of Wundt's work. Let just three points be mentioned. First, up and till today, Wundt belonged to the minority among the psychologists who realize that entirely different types of psychology will be needed to understand even approximately something of the psychic functioning of the human being. Certain aspects of that functioning may be analyzed employing approaches borrowed from or inspired by natural sciences. (To most Westerners it is obvious that without a human body, there wouldn't be psychic functioning at all, and that therefore brain research is an important auxiliary field for psychology.[6]) But other aspects of human psychic functioning are better understood when employing approaches inspired by other sciences or scholarships. (Topics central to psychology like identity, sense of self, meaning giving, and many others are far better understood by contextualizing them culturally as well as biographically and by employing methods inspired by the humanities.) Wundt explicitly stated that psychology needs to be plural and he set out himself to develop both a psychology of the human as a physiological being and a psychology of the human as a cultural being. When it comes to the psychological study of religion, Wundt was of the opinion that one should employ only cultural psychology to understand it.[7] Contrary to the tendency by most

6 Mind the formulation, however: Other people than Westerners, and even some contemporary Westerners, hold entirely different opinions!

7 Lest anyone would think I only agree with Wundt or would just sing his praises: To my opinion, Wundt exaggerated by implying that physiological (which he also called: individual) psychol-

US-psychologists to consider religion as something individual (or to be derived from something within the individual), Wundt claimed that scholarly fields like anthropology and history can teach much more about religion than psychology – and right he probably was! Secondly, Wundt also realized that these scholarly disciplines are in need of explanatory theory, however. Indeed, anthropology and history are largely descriptive types of scholarship, relying on disciplines like economy, sociology or political sciences to explain the enormous amounts of data they work with. Wundt's (like Freud's) suggestion was to also employ some psychology – a plea that remains valid right until today (Tileagă & Byford, 2014). Thirdly, different from almost everyone in whatever discussion on religion at his time, Wundt did not grant any priority to Christianity. This striving to remain neutral with regard to the core claims of any religion themselves is nowadays considered to be a prerequisite in all sciences of religions, but not in Wundt's days (and some criticized him fiercely for that reason). More radical than many present day psychologists of religion, Wundt did not even suggest that being religious is better than not being religious. (Allolio-Näcke [this volume] correctly points out, however, that Wundt's criteria for detecting historical "development" among the diverse forms of religion were hardly reflected.)

It is also very strange to read from a cultural psychologist (like Allolio-Näcke by training is) that psychology of religion would only analyze "lived" (he apparently means: "contemporary") culture. How does he call then the many analyses of cultures and cultural phenomena by psychoanalysts? Or what about the many psychohistorical studies, whether with a focus on religion or not? Do analyses like the ones offered by Erich Fromm (1950) of Buddhist versus Christian traditions belong to psychology of religion, or not? It is also odd that Allolio-Näcke (this volume) writes that psychology would deal with "culture and analyzes systems of signs, knowledge, rules and symbols" – should we not think that psychology has the psychic functioning of human beings as its focus and that some parts of psychology (loosely gathered under the label cultural psychology) draw on systems of signs, knowledge, rules, and symbols to understand that psychic functioning?

---

ogy would be of no use at all in the psychology of religion. He clearly aimed to analyze religion only as a cultural phenomenon. Correct as he was in seeing individual religiosity as derived from religion as a cultural phenomenon, he was incorrect in disregarding the possibility of exploring religiosity by means of "physiological" psychology. (On the other hand, he probably was right about limited value of this approach to understand religion as a cultural phenomenon.)

Admittedly, one can have different opinions here and much depends on definitions.

Obviously, one can have a lot of criticism, in hindsight, on Wundt. But to deny Wundt a status as psychologist of religion seems utterly unjustified.

A Strawman Fallacy?

Really more serious misunderstandings arise in or seem to be at the basis of much in Nørager's comments on *Religionspsychologie*. As he confesses, he is not a psychologist of religion himself, but a study of the psychology of his compatriot Villiam Grønbaek (1897–1970), IAPR's president between 1963 and 1969 (Nørager, 1996), qualifies him as competent reader of *Religionspsychologie*. And a skillful reader he proves himself to be! All the more surprising are some of his remarks.

Nørager insinuates that I would be looking for or even defending a single identity for "the" psychology of religion. (He even speaks of a "fixed and stable identity".) It is hard to understand where Nørager takes this from: The entire book *Religionspsychologie* (and a good deal of my other publications, which he need not be acquainted with, of course) refute the idea that there would be one single psychology of religion or that only one psychology should be accepted as psychology of religion. One of the keywords in *Religionspsychologie*, rightly noted by Nørager himself, is "Pluriformität", a German word for which no real English equivalent exist, perhaps to be translated as "plurality" or "multiplicity": psychology is plural, in many respects. And as psychology of religion can, in principle, be pursued from any psychological perspective (be it not always equally fruitful, see Belzen, 2010), by consequence this subdiscipline is plural too. Now, Nørager's text is a bit ambivalent, for he does note this view in *Religionspsychologie*. But then he claims to have detected "a certain sadness or perhaps an unwillingness to accept" this plurality or multiplicity within the psychology of religion. Of course, any reader X can claim that a text Y makes impression Z on her or him. But X should please explain what in Y evokes Z and for what reason. As is so often the case with reactions to a text, the reactions often say more about X than about Y... Mind: I do not say this as a cheap psychologizing of Nørager's impression! I have the highest opinion of Nørager's ability to read (and have repeatedly quoted his views on psychology of religion and have gladly published his excellent chapter on the correspondence between Villiam Grønbaek and Werner Gruehn; Nørager, 2000). But as he fails to say what exactly in *Religionspsychologie* evoked his *impression*, I must speculate a bit myself, happily grasping the opportunity to perhaps clarify some issues. Several things might have played a role in Nørager (this volume) getting it wrong, only four of which I will briefly comment on. (Norager's remark are sometimes of a very fundamental nature and would deserve to be taken seriously in a lengthier, systematic treatise; unfortunately, such can't be done here.)

First of all, Nørager's knowledge of IAPR's past may have led him to think that I would defend similar positions as key players in that past. Certainly there has been a tendency with Gruehn to regard Girgensohn's way of doing psychology of religion as the only, or at least as the best, psychology of religion. But this has never been the sole voice in IAPR's past. In the second half of its first century, leaders of IAPR have usual allowed for quite divers types of psychology (and sadly enough: for a period of time increasingly also for non-psychology of religion) to be present at conferences and in the *Archive*. In this respect, Nørager (this volume) seems to be reading something into *Religionspsychologie* (that is, he seems to be engaged in *eisegesis* rather than *exegesis*).

Many Other Relationships Between Psychology and Religion Than Just Psychology of Religion

Secondly, Nørager seems to have misunderstood (or perhaps wants to misunderstand… – I will come to that later, when addressing our perhaps opposing suspicions) the distinction between psychology of religion (plural in itself) on the one hand and the many other relationships between psychology and religion. And perhaps he also misunderstands my evaluation of those different kinds of relationship between psychology and religion. Let me therefore explicate: I do not think that psychology of religion (a heterogeneous enterprise) is the best, the most valuable or the most interesting of the many relationships between psychology and religion, it is *just one* of them. Psychology of religion, to give one broad (in fact: too empty) circumscription, is the effort to psychologically investigate religion. This description is "too empty" as it does not yet say anything about psychology, about what that is (and is not), it does not yet say which psychology to employ in which way, it does not say what religion is or how something called religion can be the object of a psychological investigation at all, it does not clarify whether one could or should try to investigate "religion" (in what way ever understood) or rather "religiosity" or "something religious" about the human psyche (if such a "something religious" exists at all in the human psyche) or whatever. All the issues that psychologists struggle with when they turn to "religion" as an object of research still need to be settled after having set up this empty circumscription of psychology of religion. Yet, this broad and in itself heterogeneous field is to be distinguished from other relationships between psychology and religion.

To give some examples of such other relationships: Studies concentrating on the religious character of or on the religious roots of some psychologies or on religious influences on psychology, either as a body of theory and skills or as a profession or a field, would not qualify as psychology of religion but as belonging to a field within psychology called "history and foundations of psychology" (or "history and theory of psychology" or what have you by way of equivalent). Also, the many articulations of religions, or of religious views, by way of some kind of psychology (very often another type of psychology than the one developed in the West), do usually not count as psychology of religion. Some Hindu but especially many Buddhist traditions are thoroughly psychological: Although quite different from the type of knowledge produced at Western universities and research centers for psychology, they offer some kinds of "psychology", but are themselves part and parcel of religious traditions; these psychologies therefore are "religious psychologies", they are themselves religion, whereas psychology of religion has religion as an object, it is *about* religion, but it is not religion itself (although, as granted already, religious factors in Western psychology may be detected and although religious motives are prominent in most psychology of religion).

If someone were to remark that, thus understood, psychology of religion is a mainly Western enterprise, that remark would be essentially correct. One could even add: It is a Western enterprise, practiced almost exclusively in the West, employing such psychology as being considered "scientific" in the West, and applied to religions (better: to phenomena called religious) in the West (an issue also hinted at by Zittoun, this volume). There is hardly anyone outside the West doing psychology of religion. (Just take a look at which kind of persons are on the editorial board of the media for psychology of religion: Even those few outside the West usually have been trained as psychologists in the West.)

The restriction to scientific psychology also implies that not all psychologies as developed or practiced in the West are being employed in the psychology of religion. Types of psychology by the name Parapsychology (which usually stays within a classical Western understanding of psychology) or Transpersonal Psychology (which clearly has left the boundaries of academic psychology) are hardly ever employed in the psychology of religion – for better or for worse, this is not the issue here. (Wolfradt and Demmradt, this volume, provide a welcome presentation of a rare exception.) To be sure: In the West, there have been efforts to develop more and other psychologies that could well be employed in reasoning about or in research on religion; but if they failed to have become accepted as scientific psychology on the "forum"[8], they just don't count as "scientific psychology". (Famous examples would include Otto's and von Hügel's efforts to psychologically deal with mysticism. Also remember that a great theological thinker like Schleiermacher, independently of his efforts to anchor religion in the human's being psychic nature, developed a kind of psychology of his own, well before the dawn of present day psychology and its forerunners like Helmholtz or Weber. Other than his theology, Schleiermacher's psychology never found much acceptance, not even among psychologists of religion; his efforts are hardly even remembered in circles of the history of psychology.)

Even pastoral psychology is not quite the same as psychology of religion. What is typical for pastoral psychology is its pastoral intention: The types of psychology employed in this field are the same types of psychology as employed in other psychology (and therefore the same as in psychology of religion), only it is done with a religious goal. Pastoral psychology seeks to be of benefit to pastoral work, it aims to supply the pastor with knowledge and skills for practical use in the daily work. (It is therefore an application of psychology almost exclusively practiced in the service of Christian churches, see e.g., Watts, Nye, & Savage, 2002.) Different from this cause, psychology of religion, like all the other present sciences of religions, strives to remain neutral with regard to the (theological) content of the religious phenomena studied: Psychology of religion, like the psychology of anything else in the human world (poetry, sports, organizations, etc.) has as a primary goal to investigate, to explain and perhaps understand something.

To be honest, one should realize that this in-principle-neutral stand is often as such part of a more embracing project that may have clearly religious overtones. But also in this respect, psychology of religion is not different from any other fields in applied psychology: The psychology of war, e.g., is practiced in order that the financer of the research (very often: the Pentagon) can wage war more effectively, the psychology of advertising will ultimate aim to help better sell specific products brought to the market, etc. Although psychology of religion in principle is neutral towards religious claims, one should be aware that religious agendas are almost always involved – and even if they are not,

8 As twentieth century philosophers of science (like Kuhn, Lakatos, Feyerabend, or Latour) would phrase it: Has a theory been accepted by the community of licensed practitioners, or not?

psychologists of religion usually concentrate on the religion they privately consider the most plausible or most attractive or even simply do research on the religion they happen to be raised in, see Corveleyn's and Zittoun's remarks (this volume) about psychologists of religion mainly studying their own religious orientation. The latter starting point has its own advantages and disadvantages, though, as discussed in part III of *Religionspsychologie*, to which I must refer for a lengthier treatise of this issue.

Let us take a look at only one more example of relationships between psychology and religion, other than psychology of religion. Some theologians have engaged in a kind of dialogue with some types of psychology. E.g., Paul Tillich tried to develop a "correlational method", taking psychological viewpoints, or psychological information, to understand the condition of human beings in order to find out in which way the Christian religion could respond to that condition (Tillich, 1959–1975). In many respects, there is similarity to pastoral psychology here (and the journal *Pastoral Psychology* is indeed an important medium for scholars engaged in this type of work). The differences are large as well, however. This field is highly theoretical, almost never empirical in the sense as practiced by psychologists: Although these religious thinkers have clearly an interest in empirical state of affairs, they do not engage in psychological research to find out something about that state of affairs, but they will philosophize about it, taking their information from psychological theories. It is *grand theory* that is employed here, not small scale empirical research findings as make up the majority of publications in present psychology of religion. (It has to be admitted that psychology of religion is a not very theoretical field: The call for theory and theoretical integration of the many disparate empirical findings has been heard ever since psychology of religion set out for its present quantitative growth, see, e.g., the successive editions of highly successful handbook *The Psychology of Religion: The Empirical Approach* since 1985, see also the same request repeated in the recent publication on the psychology of prayer by Spilka, the senior author of that handbook; Hood, Hill, & Spilka, 2009; Spilka, Hood, & Gorsuch, 1985; Spilka & Ladd, 2013.) Indeed, ironically perhaps, scholars engaged in what is called "the dialogue between theology and psychology" or, a bit too general, "psychology and religion", hardly ever read publications from the field of the psychology of religion; to them "psychology of religion" is at best a specific minor part of "psychology and religion" (see the organization of a volume programmatically called *Psychology and Religion: Mapping the Terrain*, Jonte-Pace & Parsons, 2001). There is a clear tendency in this field to preferably work with psychoanalytic theories, arguably one of the most theoretical approaches within Western psychology. (In some departments of religion, attention arose to quite different kind of psychology as well, however; the so-called "cognitive science of religion" draws on recent developments in neurobiology and evolutionary psychology [Feierman, 2009; Geertz, 2010; Wilson, Bulbulia, & Sibley, 2014]; in many respects this fairly new field of "cognitive science of religion" resembles the psychology of religion in its early years; although its practitioners are usually not trained as psychologists, there is hardly overlap between the practitioners of both fields – for better or for worse, that is not at stake here.)

Nørager is clearly confusing "psychology of religion" on the one hand and "psychology and religion" on the other hand when he is expressing his preference for "the attempt to establish constructive, academic dialogue between the world of psychology and the world of religion". As just explained, to some extent, such an attempt does exist already, it is, in the USA, often called "psychology and religion". Nørager is free, of course, to prefer this field to the psychology of religion as it presents itself in its publications and networks, and it is quite understandable that a systematic theologian who has developed into a philosopher of religion like Nørager prefers something theoretical like "psychology and religion" to the often all-too-small scale empirical psychology of religion.

Science is Not Identical to What It is About

There may, however, be a third issue responsible for misunderstandings between Nørager and me, namely the distinction between science or scholarship on the one hand and some aspect of the reality that science and scholarship are supposed to deal with on the other hand. To help to explain, let us turn to an example. To most people, many flowers are beautiful. The beauty involved here is another beauty than the beauty of, e.g., a biological theory that can explain a good number of things about that flower: Why does it grow where it is, how does it grow, how does it spread, which dangers exist to that flower, etc. There is a fundamental difference, however, between a biological theory about, e.g., a flower and that flower itself. A biological theory is scientific device: It aims to investigate, analyze and understand certain aspects of that flower, but it remains silent about other things, equally true or important, that may be said about that flower. Whether the flower is beautiful, is not an issue for the biologist; what the flower would cost if purchased in a shop, is not an issue for a biologist; what poetry may have been inspired by the flower or what use is made of the flower in poetry, is not issue for the biologist; whether the flower can be regarded as part of a divine creation, is not an issue for a biologist. What biology can find out and say about the flower is very limited, but also very important: Perhaps the flower is dangerous to human species and biology can explain how; but perhaps the flower can, under certain conditions, also be used to produce some medicine; perhaps we would like to have more of that flower; biology can help to explain how and why and consequently how to proceed if we want to cultivate the flower. Furthermore, the kind of knowledge provided by biology, or by any other science, is also unique: not to be had anywhere else. A poet or a theologian cannot answer the kind of questions dealt with by, e.g., biology (nor the other way round: A biologist need not professionally know about poetry or theology). The value granted to the kind of knowledge provided by the biologist (or by anyone else) will vary, depending on the kind of context in which people deal with that flower: To someone wanting to send flowers to a lover the biological aspects of the flower will not matter, but its financial value may well matter; to a biologist the use of the flower in poetry or in a painting may be insignificant, but not an art historian. Et cetera. To reiterate: There is a fundamental distinction between different kinds of knowledge and also between knowledge on the one hand and what that knowledge is assumed to be about on the other hand.

Perhaps other than Nørager (this volume) assumes, psychology is part of science and scholarship, it provides some kind of knowledge that is unique and cannot be obtained anywhere, knowledge that – if proved sound – can be very powerful, but that is, of course, also limited, and its value will depend on the context. Sometimes, some kind of psychological knowledge seems to have been available already to great thinkers and artists in the past, but more often than not this is really just an impression. Granted, the sensitivity to emotional factors in human life seems to have been with some poets all the time. Yet, on a closer view, such knowledge is usually of a quite different kind, the knowledge of the poet having more to do with individual talent or genius and with intuition, the scientific knowledge on the contrary being by definition not individual at all: Scientific knowledge is not intuitive, but systematic, available to all with the training required and it will only count as scientific knowledge if accepted by a relevant community of scholars (the "forum" hinted at above already).

Religious experiences (or better: experiences called religious by some people at a certain time and at a certain place) have been phrased in numerous ways, also in artistic ways. Sometimes, religious experiences have inspired works of art, sometimes they have prompted scientific investigations. But works of art are not the same as scientific work (as will hopefully need no explanation), they require different training and will be evaluated differently, depending on the context. What science can tell us about religious experiences will be a specific type of information, scientific information, in itself limited, but not to be had anywhere else, and of a value that will depend on the context in which some kind of information is required. Psychology as part of science and scholarship will and can only answer some questions about some aspects of religious experiences. Moreover, the kind of information provided by the different types of psychology is different too and to many observers it will be questionable what the value is at all of psychological information about religious experiences. It should be an important caveat to psychologists that after initial enthusiasm (around, say, 1900) by theologians and other scholars on religions (e.g., historians of religion) about the kind of information to be obtained from psychology, they since decades have largely lost their interest: Psychology of religion clearly is a growing field, but mainly due to the ever increasing number of psychologists, not because theologians and religionists would be especially impressed by what psychologists have to tell about religion and therefore would engage psychologists of religion. Compare: At departments for theology, for religion, for religious studies, or however they may be called, there is hardly any teaching in the psychology of religion. (And if there is, it is usually only psychoanalytic perspectives that are being dealt with, so precisely that type of psychological knowledge that at present is being eliminated from what is regarded as scientific psychology by the "forum" of psychologists – for better or for worse, again, that is not at stake here.) At a few departments of religion, notably in the USA, there is interest in something like a "theology and psychology-dialogue", but, as noted already, this is not be identified with psychology of religion.

If this modest perspective on the psychology of religion makes to Nørager (this volume) the impression of being "sad", so be it. I don't see any sadness here. I try to see psychology (better, of course: the ensemble of approaches and practitioners that count as "psychological" at a certain time and place) as realistically as possible. The knowledge about human beings, also in their psychic aspects, and the insight into the *condition humaine* as articulated by artists, philosophers, and also sometimes by religious geniuses (often at the same time artists or philosophers as well) may (and does) count to many observers as deeper, more fundamental or anything than what psychologists find out, but if a piece of *scientific* psychological knowledge is sound and valid knowledge, it is knowledge not to be had anywhere else (also not from artists or philosophers), valuable in its own right, but valued different, depending on the context of that evaluation. (At a funeral, a poem on bereavement will certainly be more appropriate than the reading of a paper reporting some psychological research on some aspect of bereavement.)[9]

9 Perhaps here I should also comment briefly on Corveleyn's kindly writing about my "nearly

I grant that I do not join the to my taste oftentimes too enthusiastic talk about psychology or by psychologists, aiming to promote the profession's cause (or perhaps the cause of an organization making money on psychology like the divers national associations for psychology). Also, I do not try to obtain from psychology the answers to questions that may be the questions that interest many people more than do the proper psychological questions. When it comes to religion, many people expect that psychology can tell why human beings are religious, what religion is good for, whether a religious experience is real or not, whether religion heals or damages or is perhaps itself a manifestation of some kind of psychic (dys)functioning. But whether people should be religious or not, and in what way they should be so, is not for psychology to tell. (And even if psychology would find out that being religious in tradition A is higher correlated with indicators for health than being religious in tradition B, this still would not necessarily imply that A is true or better than B, it would just tell that people following tradition A have a higher statistical change of being healthy – in itself, according to most religious and humanist traditions, not an ultimate value! – than people following tradition B.) Likewise, quite a bit of research reported is presented as "psychological knowledge", but in fact all kinds of findings by means of questionnaires and even tests as devised by psychologists do not achieve much more than to provide an inventory of opinions found with a certain sample at a certain time and place. Therefore, one should not expect more from psychology than psychology can give: At best, psychology can add to our knowledge about the human being, more precisely, to our knowledge of certain aspects of the psychic functioning of human beings, also when it comes to religion. By logical consequence, the state of affairs in psychology at large is found back in psychology of religion as well: There are many schools, approaches, theories, methods and techniques in psychology, almost all of which could be employed and increasingly are being employed in psychology of religion.

loving attention" for the psychology of religion (this volume). Obviously, close attention may reveal a kind of "love". To me, psychology of religion is a very interesting field and although at present an academic job in the Netherland is not much fun, I have always regarded it a privilege to have found professional employment in this field. Had I been employed in another field, however – decades ago, an old friend of mine wanted me to join him in importing furniture – I might well have given "nearly loving attention" to that field too, probably, as I try to do my job as properly as possible.

What Kind of Progress in Psychology of Religion?

To some observers, this last point will clearly count as progress for the psychology of religion: a larger number of perspectives is employed, the discrepancy between psychology at large on the one hand and psychology of religion on the other hand that for decades has been lamented by leaders of the field since, say, the 1960s, is decreasing, there is now a higher likelihood to get research on religion published in psychology journals not devoted to the psychology of religion only. One should not underestimate these developments: It is for psychology of religion of vital importance to remain in touch with the motherdiscipline of psychology, which necessarily means that it is vital to be accepted on the "forum" of psychology (although one should never forget that this "forum" is constituted in a particular way at a certain time and in a certain place – there being no stable "forum" for any science is a characteristic of the ever changing nature of scientific knowledge). To evaluate "the" psychology of religion will be as complicated as to evaluate "the" psychology at large, it may be best to be aware of very different criteria that could be employed. As should be clear from turning to most so-called "handbooks" in psychology, there is no such thing as one and single psychology, therefore is not one and single psychology of religion either. Yet, whatever its value, psychology of religion is *psychology* of religion (as tautologically, and to some perhaps controversial, as that may sound). To know what psychology is, we will need to turn to the forum of psychology, to know what religion is, one will need to turn to another forum (therefore, what counts as psychology or as religion will be different at different times and places).

But in any case one needs to continue to distinguish between science (including psychology) and what is it supposed to be about. Psychology is about psychic functioning, also when it comes to religion (and therefore a psychology of religion can exist). Psychology can be *about* religion, but psychology does not *dialogue* with religion. Not religion, not the rituals performed by people, not the experiences made by religious people are psychology's partner in dialogue: Psychology as a scientific enterprise can be about these experiences, but it does not converse with them. (Psychology does not converse with art, with war, with advertising, what have you either: It is about such things. But psychology, obviously, can be in dialogue with other sciences about the same empirical reality, and psychologists can share their findings with others interested, for whatever reason, in art, war, advertising, etc.) Next to being too general (as noted above), the label "psychology and religion" is therefore a bit confusing, the better phrasing was "the dialogue between theology and psychology" (Homans, 1968). Of course, psychologists can have a dialogue with theologians and religious scholars, and of course, psychologists may privately voice religious opinions. But contrary to what Nørager (this volume) says, "moving freely between religious self-descriptions and scientific distance" cannot be an ideal to any scholarly enterprise: Scholarship is characterized primarily by its being systematic, by its taking a very specific and strict method in approaching any issue. Mixing up statements of totally different kinds does not build up any science. In the history of many sciences, it has taken some time to learn to distinguish between religious propositions, empirical descriptions, theoretical statements and others. (Sentences in Genesis 1, e.g., do not add to our knowledge about the earth's history or about the evolution of life on that planet.) Contrary to what has been claimed in the past, there is no religious science (but there is a religious use of science, there is science practiced by religious people or in religious institutions, etc.). Just as there is no religious physics, there is – according to Western understanding of science – no religious psychology. One cannot base the psychology one is developing on religious claims; on the contrary, one should base psychology on empirical observations and then perhaps apply it to religious phenomena, including religious claims. William James, apparently admired so much by Nørager, did not do what Nørager (this volume) suggests James did: He did not build up his psychology on a mixture of religious self-descriptions and scientific observations. His magisterial work *The Principals of Psychology* (James, 1890), which may well be regarded as psychology's instigating publication, was not based on religious self-descriptions at all. And in *The Varieties of Religious Experience* (James, 1902/2002) is not speaking as a psychologist, but – as he explicitly states – as a philosopher, who wants to base himself on empirical observations. James' aim in *The Varieties* was to come up with a *philosophy* of religion, not a psychology of religion; the entire *Varieties* is a neatly organized exposé of religious experiences, about which James wanted to develop a philosophy (what he never did, however). The *Varieties* is a highly readable work, for good reasons a bestseller, its importance existing in being one of the first to talk about religious experiences not from a religious perspective, but from an empirical perspective. (One can hardly overestimate this point: Even today, a large number, perhaps even a majority of Westerners start talking religiously, even if anti-religiously, when they say something about religion. To be able to deal with religion, in the context of science and scholarship, is not so easy: It requires leaving aside religious – or for that sake, anti-religious – sympathies and restricting oneself to the perspective of the science one claims to be practicing. And as Holm (this volume) points out so eloquently, it is oftentimes is not easy to remain able to handle, each in their own right, a religious perspective next to a scientific perspective – as opposed to identifying or mixing them.)

Also, I doubt whether "a study of God-talk in popular music would be a worth-while empirical task for future psychology of religion". What would be the use of such an investigation? What would be psychological about it? That "heart language", as Nørager (this volume) calls some folk psychology, is certainly often much more beautiful and seemingly better fitting than any psychological treatise about emotions or anything, I will grant immediately: Science is no poetry, the beauty of a scientific theory (if what is meant here is correctly called "beauty") is very different from the beauty we encounter in art (including poetry). And that scientific psychology is, at present, often hardly able to say more, or better or even only more precise, than other discourses, I needed to conclude myself in the *Archive for the Psychology of Religion* when considering why religious music is often so moving to listeners, even to the extent of turning atheists into a kind of believers for the time of the music sounding (Belzen, 2013). But all of this does not imply that we should be "moving freely between religious self-descriptions and scientific distance"; rather, what we should do is analyze such religious self-descriptions from a scientific distance. Nor does it not mean we should weave religious propositions into the construction of any scientific knowledge: scientific knowledge is precise, even supreme, within its specific perspective – but authoritative only within that perspective![10] The increasing disentanglement of religious and scientific claims and propositions is usually seen as a kind of progress, as is the clearer understanding of the *proprium* of such claims and propositions; giving in to

10 Being precise also prevents jumping to (wishful) conclusions as Nørager (this volume) seems to be doing. From the observation that in "heart language", "folk model[s] of the mind", like in love songs, there sometimes are references to "God", Nørager wants to conclude "that there is a close, internal connection between *religion* (or better: religious longing) and human *love*". That is unsound reasoning, however. What we can conclude is that in some "heart language" the word "God" is employed. One could investigate which kind of religious language has since when and under what conditions been employed in love songs; one surely will detect, in a Western contexts, traces of the Judeo-Christian tradition in all kind of art (incl. poetry), but all that does not that imply a "close, internal connection" between religion and human love. On the contrary: Religious language decreasingly employed in love songs should count as an indication that such a connection does not exist! Love songs just employ some of the metaphors available in a certain culture context, and therefore sometimes one also finds religious metaphors employed. Some theologian or religionists may want to arrive at a conclusion as suggested by Nørager, but a scientist can't side with them.

Nørager's desire would, from this perspective, be a step back. (And I also don't understand at all from where Nørager takes it that I would like to throw psychoanalytic perspectives out of the window: In both *Religionspsychologie* and in the rest of my work there is high appreciation of psychoanalysis, Erikson has always been one of the my favorites and psychohistory has been a major part of my own program in the psychology of religion [Belzen, 2001, 2004; Belzen & Geels, 2008]! And by the way: The kind of hypotheses as necessary in clinical work, e.g., in diagnosing, or in interpreting empirical data or in developing a theory is not all "speculative" in the sense as suggested by Nørager.)

A Multidimensional Model Becoming as Complex as Its Empirical Referent

A fourth thing that Nørager may have missed is perhaps my not identifying psychology with everything-that-is-said-or-done-by-psychologists. Obviously (hopefully), private opinions of a psychologist do not count as psychological knowledge. Many evaluations by psychologists are not founded in psychological knowledge either, but are the result of their inculturation at a certain time and place, of their political, economic, even religious taste or preference.[11] As already noted above, not all that psychologists report on is psychological work. Neither is psychology to be restricted to psychologists. Although it is good and fair that nowadays there exist a requirement to be licensed as a psychologists to do certain psychological work, it also remains true that anyone else than a psychologist might come up with some bit of psychological finding or insight – the "forum" will judge, and it would a silly forum if it would only grant the right to formulate psychological findings to licensed psychologists. (It would nowadays probably take such an "anyone-else-than-a-psychologist" an equally long time as the training as psychologist to be become acquainted with psychological knowledge and skills, but in principle it remains possible for such an "anyone-else-than-a-psychologist" to set out doing a piece of psychological research or to come up with a genuine psychological interpretation.) Especially

11 As a matter of fact, such non-psychological findings often cause important biases, also in psychological work, and result in knowledge presented as scientific while in fact being articulations of the author's prejudices. Note, however, that sometimes prejudices can be very worthwhile, even in scientific work – the most well-known concept in psychology of religion, most frequently employed in research (the distinction between intrinsic and extrinsic religion), is owed to Allport's being religiously prejudiced (Allport, 1950). Also note that it is sometimes very hard to distinguish between prejudices and scientific claims.

in the realm of applied psychology, where the primary aim is not the generation of new, additional scientific psychological knowledge, but the bringing existing psychological knowledge into interaction with a certain state of affairs, it happens often enough that people with training in that certain field are better equipped to bring psychology to bear on that field than psychologists without knowledge of that specific field. The psychology of literature or of any other art is more often than not practiced by people with initial training in literature studies etc. (but of course such scholars will need some type of studying psychology in order to be able to practice some psychology, only they do not necessarily need a diploma or other professional qualification as psychologist). The same holds for the psychology of religion: It is not any longer a matter of some reading or by absolving some short course that one can become a psychologist and then get involved in psychology of religion (as was in the days of the founding fathers of present day psychology of religion). But there are excellent colleagues in the psychology of religion who never made any formal diploma in academic psychology and nevertheless come up with sound psychological interpretations and findings. People like Antoon Vergote or André Godin (1905–1997), also figuring in IAPR's past, or Don Capps (1939–2015), who remained an outsider to IAPR, may now count as (recent) historical examples. However, perhaps Nørager and I share some suspicions, but only of an opposite nature: Whereas he suspects that I want to restrict the label psychology of religion to formally qualified psychologists, I suspect by overstretching that same label he wants to give non-psychologists the opportunity to present themselves as psychologists…

In general, one can think of a fundamental science a being a complex of concentric circles: The development of new or better knowledge about what a specific science is supposed to be about (in our case: the very object of psychology), would be the center. In the first circle around that center one finds the efforts to theoretically conceptualize that object. (Obviously, in the perspective of different psychological theories, this first circle looks differently, primarily as a result of a different opinion about how to determine psychology's object.) Around this circle, there is a next, thin one, home to methodology: to the theoretical reflection on what kind of methods and techniques to develop and to employ in order to investigate the very center of the circle. A much wider circle contains, in the case of psychology, all kinds of research into the psychic aspects of human functioning and its results in a variety of contexts. A fourth circle presents all kinds of practical application of psychological knowledge in settings like clinical work and counseling, organizational work, pedagogy, and many more. In the fifth circle are located all kinds of relationships to domains and other sciences that don't need psychology to exist, but that in order to function better do take into account what psychology may have to tell. Medicine in a narrow sense, e.g., does not need psychology, yet psychological factors do matter in medical work (and their impact is only gradually acknowledged at present); in a field like ethics, it would be unwise to neglect what psychology may have to tell about human beings. Finally, one could imagine an even larger sixth circle in which psychology's place in society, in social discourse, is situated: psychology has impact, for better or for worse, on the public opinion, psychology shapes the perspective of participants in Western societies, psychology has made its way into common parlance, etc. Mind that all of this is only a model, just a way of depicting the whole of psychology, therefore necessary limited (and therefore incomplete and flawed as any model is, since no model can replace reality itself). One needs to realize that not only do different opinions exist about the core of the entire enterprise, but that other sciences have sometimes their say about that same core too: Whether determined as "subjectivity", "behavior", "psychic functioning" or whatever, disciplines like history or sociology have something to say about psychology's core too, and any embracing psychology is drawing on a great number of other sciences, like neurology or genetics, to reflect on its very object, in what way ever conceptualized. If one would like to depict all of this, one would need to draw a picture of the models of different sciences, each aiming at empirical reality, interacting with one another and with all kinds of influences. Even though still not reality itself, obviously, such a picture would become as complicated as a drawing by Escher ...

Complex as all of this may sound, it is still far too simple, especially when it comes to an applied field in psychology, like the psychology of religion. Such a subdiscipline, in which psychology is brought to bear on another field (sports, war, whatever) needs a double focus, it is therefore not shaped like a circle, but like an ellipse. One of the focuses is with psychology, the other one, in the case of psychology of religion, with religion. Even if one would want to pursue it from a monodisciplinary perspective, e.g., from a neuropsychological or attachment perspective only, as a practitioner one also needs profound knowledge of the empirical object one is turning to, even if only to be able to ask appropriate questions. Just handing out a questionnaire to any members of some religious organizations is not likely to produce much insight into anything religious. If one would want to do research about, e.g., prayer, one will need to know what prayer is or means within the tradition a person x belongs. Nils Holm (this volume) provides a fine example: In order to find out something meaningful about behavior called glossolalia, one will need to consider whether one is dealing with subjects from a Christian tradition, one will need to take into account the biblically inspired meaning glossolalia has within the various

Christian churches, etc. Glossolalia being preferred in Pentecostal churches but hardly ever found in Roman Catholic churches apriori implies that the apparently same, or least similar behavior, will be structured psychologically differently for followers of such different religious traditions. Whereas in one tradition it might be contributing to mental health, in another it may be a symptom of mental illness (Griffith, 2010).

Being involved in a field with a double focus, psychologists of religion also need to take into account what other disciplines have to say about religion. Psychologists do not just need such knowledge on behalf of an empirical investigation of a specific religious phenomenon; in order to come up with profound reflection they also need to consider the theoretical issues about religion as raised by other branches of scholarship. (To take a simple example: Although psychologists don't need to develop their own definitions of religion, they should be aware of the problematic nature of such definitions, they should know about their limits, about the probably limited generalizability of their findings and interpretations, etc.) To remind of another truism: It is hard to conceive of sound psychology of religion if its practitioners do not keep in mind the changing nature of what is called religion throughout human history and if they do not listen to what other scholars on religion bring to the fore about that elusive object, religion.[12]

As a consequence, it is not so easy to establish a clear demarcation between psychology of religion and the fields it relates to. There is not much use in employing a rigid either-or kind of thinking. Zittoun (this volume), e.g., is very correct in pointing out that there is a theoretical aspect to work in the psychology of religion: For sure, psychology of religion is the employment of existing

12 For a more sophisticated discussion of this multidimensional model of psychology of religion, see Belzen (2007). Note that psychology of religion, viewed this way, can be seen both a subdiscipline of psychology and of what Germans would call "Religionswissenschaften" (the ensemble of all sciences on religion). Ideally, a practitioner of the psychology of religion will be qualified in both fields (as in the past, it so often has been the case!). When having only diploma's in psychology, the psychologist of religion should make sure she gets expert knowledge about "religion" (about both specific cases and about theoretical discourse), when having only diploma's in theology and/or Religious Studies, the psychologist of religion should make sure she gets expert knowledge about the different theories in psychology and acquaint herself with its diverse empirical techniques. At present, it has to be admitted, the large majority of psychologists of religion in trained only in some kind of psychology; there is hardly anyone from the Religious Studies-side to have taken the time and pain to get acquainted with psychological empirical research. Without boasting: IAPR's presidents in the recent past (including the presence) all were fully licensed in both fields!

psychology in the exploration of an empirical phenomenon called religious, but in the end, such exploration will not only tell us something about that religious phenomenon, but also about the psychology employed. As discussed above, psychology of religion is no religious psychology, the psychology employed does not need to be applied to religion to be or become a valid psychology. But ultimately, when a certain psychology is well established, we will always ask for its theoretical *portée*, we will want to know to what extent it is able to cover the full width of being human. And if a psychology is, ultimately, not able to say anything at all about something so specific for human beings as religion, it must probably be deemed a poor psychology (see also Belzen, 2008). Zittoun's (this volume) reminding that psychology of religion should remain (or become again) a partner in "wider and foundational debates in psychology, as it once was the case" is to be taken equally seriously.

In the light of this desideratum even the existence of separate journals for the psychology of religion must be looked critically at. Evidently, there are advantages in having such journals, as it may help to get work in this field published. Preferably, however, a piece in the psychology of religion should be sound psychology and therefore publishable in any appropriate psychology journal. The latter allows to a much greater extent for impact within psychology at large and for discussion with the rest of psychology instead of only among psychologists of religion! As we have to realize so often (see Belzen, 2015; this issue), what counts as an advantage or as progress in one respect, may be a disadvantage or even regression in another respect. Easy one-liners should be left to commercials and bad journalism, scholarly reflection goes for nuance and depth of thought.

Final Words

Quite a number of issues have been raised by the contributors to this volume reflecting on the psychology of religion as present in the context of its International Association, far more than could be dealt with in this short Afterword. Nevertheless, I trust that after the reflections offered above, the answer to the only question explicitly formulated in the preceding chapters can be brief. Nørager (this volume) asks whether it is "conceivable that Wobbermin may have a valid point" in criticizing psychology of religion for not having much (perhaps even nothing) to tell about religion as such; according to Wobbermin, most (or perhaps all) psychology of religion would be just psychology applied to religious phenomena. Again, it is somewhat puzzling that this question is raised by someone who read *Religionspsychologie*, for as I pointed out there (and in the introduction to this special issue as well), I think this is true for a larger part of the publications in the psychology of religion ("illustration and application" of psychology, as I called it). But that larger part is not the entire psychology of religion! There is also its counterpart, very theoretical, very fascinating, but exaggerating by not explaining too little, but too much: It is and cannot be the task of a single science like psychology to explain all of religion. To think like this is plainly a case of illegitimate reductionism. Yet both parts aim to contribute to the exploration of specific religious phenomena by letting psychology's partial light shine on them and to discuss religious phenomena in the light of psychology, thereby contributing to their understanding, which remains a very important, perhaps the most important task of the psychology of religion.

In the perspective of the multidimensional model shortly presented above, neither Gustav Vorbrodt (1860–1929) nor Georg Wobbermin (1869–1943), two German theologians around 1900 interested in a psychological approach to religion, belonged to the core representatives of the psychology of religion, but obviously they both belong to its broader history. Vorbrodt called for an empirical-psychological approach, but what he proposed as such himself has never been accepted by anyone, not even by such scholars as were entirely in favor of his theoretical plea. He was a forerunner of both the psychology of religion as a subdiscipline, of its International Association and of the *Archive for Psychology of Religion*: He helped to establish infrastructure, he helped to stir up interest in the psychology of religion, but never practiced it himself. Likewise, Wobbermin explicitly stated he wanted to raise appetite for the psychology of religion in Germany – and certainly he did! Being exceptionally well read in the psychology of religion of his days, he in many reviews informed a broad readership about what was going on in this field. He wanted to base an entire theology on something he called "psychology of religion" or a "transcendental psychology of religion-method", but it wasn't accepted by anyone as psychology of religion as it had, in the judgment of both his contemporaries and his later commentators, no resemblance to any psychology at all. However, the discussion (better: the fight) between Vorbrodt and Wobbermin about what is under which conditions appropriately called psychology of religion and about what kind of methods should be employed in this field, does belong to theoretical psychology of religion, as it belongs, in the model presented above, to the circle of "methodological reflection", even if both of them did not do empirical work in the psychology of religion, neither in research nor in counseling or in any other respect.

Psychology of religion is a heterogeneous enterprise. Although one may embrace a broad circumscription of this field, not everything between the poles psychology and religion belongs to the field. The field has its strengths and its weaknesses, its opportunities and its limits. It is a fascinating field, full of promise, but it is not a simple field; it is neither easy to conceive nor to practice. Throughout the first century of its International Association we have slowly learned to understand what it possibly could be: a scientifically precise, but limited approach to additional, i.e., psychological, understanding of empirical state of affairs called (by some at some time and some place) religious. And we have witnessed in this history all kinds of all too human factors (including tragedies). In a way, the psychology of religion, now perhaps (hopefully!) having overcome a number of childhood diseases, is still at the beginning of its history. But still being young, it may grow up and mature. For sure, its history will continue to be fascinating and full of surprises. From what we now know about that history, the subdisciple has probably only just started. Together with numerous other scientific disciplines, it may help us to come to some understanding of what it is assumed to be about: the human phenomena called religion. Let us wish the field, its International Association, and the *Archive* a good future!

References

Allport, G. W. (1950). *The individual and his religion: A psychological interpretation.* New York: Macmillan.

Belzen, J. A. (Ed.). (2001). *Psychohistory in psychology of religion: Interdisciplinary studies.* Amsterdam/Atlanta: Rodopi.

Belzen, J. A. (2004). *Religie, melancholie en zelf. Een historische en psychologische studie over een psychiatrisch ego-document uit de negentiende eeuw.* Kampen: Kok.

Belzen, J. A. (2007). *Psychologie en het raadsel van de religie. Beschouwingen bij een eeuw godsdienstpsychologie in Nederland.* Amsterdam: Boom.

Belzen, J. A. (2008, December 10). Über Religionspsychologie: Konditionen und Gründe ihrer Existenz. *Journal für Psychologie, 16*(3), Article 02. Retrieved December 10, 2008, from <http://www.journal-fuer-psychologie.de/jfp-3-2008-02.html>.

Belzen, J. A. (2010). *Towards cultural psychology of religion. Principles, approaches, applications.* Dordrecht/Heidelberg/London/New York: Springer.

Belzen, J. A. (2013). Music and religion: Psychological perspectives and their limits. *Archiv für Religionspsychologie, 35*, 1–29.

Belzen, J. A. (2015). *Religionspsychologie. Eine historische Analyse im Spiegel der Internationalen Gesellschaft.* Heidelberg/Berlin: Springer.

Belzen, J. A., & Geels, A. (Eds.). (2008). *Autobiography and the psychological study of religious lives.* Amsterdam/New York: Rodopi.

Feierman, J. R. (2009). *The biology of religious behavior: The evolutionary origins of faith and religion*. Santa Barbara, CA/Oxford, England: Praeger.

Fromm, E. (1950). *Psychoanalysis and religion*. New Haven, CN: Yale University Press.

Geertz, A. W. (2010). Too much mind and not enough brain, body and culture: On what needs to be done in the cognitive science of religion. *Historia Religionum*, 2, 21–37.

Griffith, J. L. (2010). *Religion that heals, religion that harms. A guide for clinical practice*. New York/London: Guilford.

Heine, S. (2005). *Grundlagen der Religionspsychologie: Modelle und Methoden*. Göttingen: Vandenhoeck & Ruprecht.

Homans, P. (1968). *The dialogue between theology and psychology*. Chicago: University of Chicago Press.

Hood, R. W., Hill, P. C., & Spilka, B. (2009). *The psychology of religion: An empirical approach* (4th ed.). New York: Guilford.

James, W. (1890). *The principles of psychology*. London: MacMillan.

James, W. (1902/2002). *The varieties of religious experience: A study in human nature*. London/New York: Routledge.

Jonte-Pace, D., & Parsons, W. B. (Eds.). (2001), *Religion and psychology: Mapping the terrain*. New York/London: Routledge.

Klünker, W. U. (1985). *Psychologische Analyse und theologische Wahrheit: Die religionspsychologische Methode Georg Wobbermins*. Göttingen: Vandenhoeck & Ruprecht.

Machoń, (H). (2005). *Religiöse Erfahrung zwischen Emotion und Kognition. William James', Karl Girgensohns, Rudolf Ottos und Carl Gustav Jungs Psychologie des religiösen Erlebens*. München: Utz.

Nestler, E. (1986). *Der Beitrag Wilhelm Stählins zur Jugendbewegung*. (Dissertation Bayreuth)

Nørager, T. (1996). *Hjerte og Psyke. Studier i den religiøse oplevens metapsykologi og diskurs*. [Heart and Psyche: Studies on the Metapsychology and Discourse of Religious Experience]. København: Forlaget Anis.

Nørager, T. (2000). Villiam Grønbaek and the Dorpat School: Elements of a 'history' based on the correspondence between Villiam Grønbaek and Werner Gruehn. In J. A. Belzen (Ed.), *Aspects in contexts – Studies in the history of psychology of religion*, (pp. 173–233). Amsterdam/Atlanta, GA: Rodopi.

Parsons, W. B. (1999) *The enigma of the oceanic feeling: Revisioning the psychoanalytic theory of mysticism*. New York: Oxford University Press.

Parsons, W. B. (2013). *Freud and Augustine in dialogue: Psychoanalysis*, mysticism, and the culture of modern spirituality*. Charlottesville/London: The University of Virginia Press.

Spilka, B., Hood, R. W., & Gorsuch, R. L. (1985). *The psychology of religion: An empirical approach*. Englewood Cliffs, NJ: Prentice-Hall.

Spilka, B., & Ladd, K. L. (2013). *The psychology of prayer: A scientific approach*. New York/London: Guilford.

Tileagă, C., & Byford, J. (Eds.). (2014). *Psychology and history. Interdisciplinary explorations*. Cambridge: Cambridge University Press.

Tillich, P. (1959–1975). *Gesammelte Werke* [Collected Works]. Stuttgart: Evangelisches Verlagswerk.

Vandermeersch, P., & Westerink, H. (2007). *Godsdienstpsychologie in cultuurhistorisch perspectief*. Amsterdam: Boom.

Vergote, A. (1966/1967). *Godsdienstpsychologie* [Psychology of Religion]. Tielt: Lannoo.

Vergote, A. (1984/1997). *Religion, belief and unbelief. A psychological study*. Amsterdam/ Atlanta, GA: Rodopi.

Vergote, A. (2000). De toekomstige godsdienstpsychologie. In J. A. Belzen (Ed.), *Op weg naar morgen. Godsdienstpsychologie in Nederland. Teksten II* (pp 178–193). Kampen: Kok.

Watts, F., Nye, R., & Savage, S. (2002). *Psychology for Christian ministry*. London/New York: Routledge.

Wilson, M. S., Bulbulia, J., & Sibley, C. G. (2014). Differences and similarities in religious and paranormal beliefs: A typology of distinct faith signatures. *Religion, Brain & Behavior, 4*(2), 104–126.

Wulff, D. M. (1991). *Psychology of religion: Classic and contemporary views*. New York: Wiley.

Printed in the United States
By Bookmasters